IMAGES of America
JOHN'S ISLAND

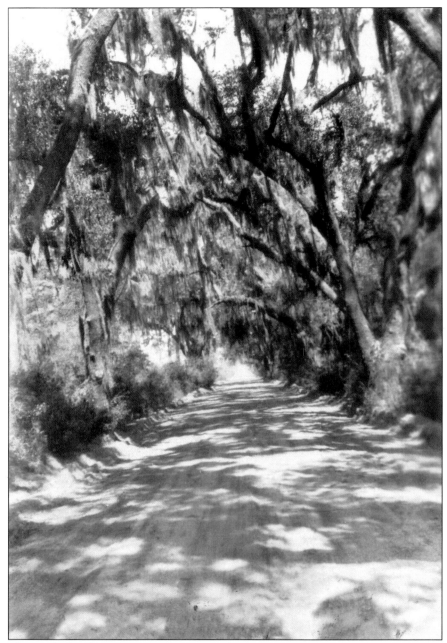

Once a footpath for the Native Americans, Bohicket Road, named after the tribes, was once used by troops in the Revolutionary War and the Civil War. It was designated a scenic highway by the South Carolina legislature on July 9, 1974. This photograph of a stretch near Acorn Hill plantation was taken prior to its paving in 1949.

ON THE COVER: Growing up around the water has always been part of John's Island life. Pictured on Church Creek in this early-1900s photograph are Joe Jim Hart, Pauline Hanahan, Evelyn Hart, Marie Hanahan, Erline Hart, and their friend Martha. (Courtesy of Joe and Henry Rivers.)

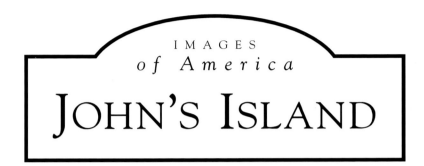

IMAGES of America
JOHN'S ISLAND

Connie Walpole Haynie

Copyright © 2007 by Connie Walpole Haynie
ISBN 978-0-7385-4346-8

Published by Arcadia Publishing
Charleston, South Carolina

Printed in the United States of America

Library of Congress Catalog Card Number: 2006930540

For all general information contact Arcadia Publishing at:
Telephone 843-853-2070
Fax 843-853-0044
E-mail sales@arcadiapublishing.com
For customer service and orders:
Toll-Free 1-888-313-2665

Visit us on the Internet at www.arcadiapublishing.com

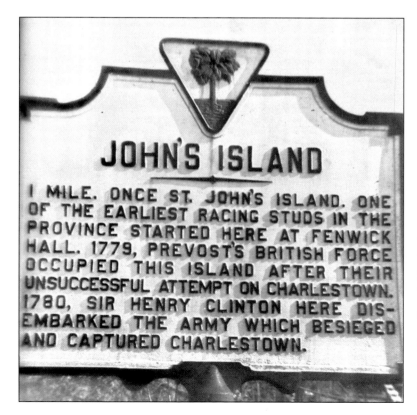

The John's Island mile marker, which once stood on Main Road off Highway 17, bore the historic spelling of the island, which was named for St. John's Parish in Barbados by the first English settlers who had lived there.

CONTENTS

Acknowledgments		6
Introduction		7
1.	The First Planters	9
2.	Seeds of War	21
3.	Fields of Destruction	27
4.	The Hardscrabble Years	43
5.	Planting New Ideas	77
6.	Harvest of Change	105
7.	Growing Developments	119

Acknowledgments

This book is dedicated to the community of John's Island with appreciation and gratitude to those who graciously shared their photographs and stories. Unfortunately, all the great pictures and stories contributed could not be included, but if the book only inspires the present generation to record their memories and family histories for the future, then it has accomplished enough. Photographs were contributed by Henry and Carmen Rivers, Joe and Johnnie Rivers, June Walpole Dickerson, Margaret Seabrook, Grey and Anne G. Minshew, Billy and Mary Hills, Ethel Nepveux, Linda Legare Berry and family, Betty Stringfellow, Marion and Annie Caroline Reid, Ben and Lisa Walpole, Kay Williams, Gordon and Charlotte Hay, H2Osmosis, Bud Hay, Lydia Hay Pedersen, Lyle Browning, Cheryl English, Charleston Aviation Authority, the Episcopal Diocese of South Carolina, the Catholic Diocese of Charleston, John and Teddy Walpole, Gene and Estelle Walpole, Legare and Aileen Walpole, Rev. Bobby Taylor, Rev. Robin Deas, Bob and Jane Biggerstaff, Eleanor Jenkins, Bill Jenkins, Tommy Townsend, Jack and Andrea Limehouse, Nancy L. Carter, Grey Geissler, Frank and Elaine Howard, Doris Hardy, Alma and Robbie LaRoche and family, Jane Jenkins Herlong, Ada Rast, Catherine Grimshaw, Claire Glover, Elizabeth Gatch Blitch, Rene Saunders, Ernest and Annie L. Koger, Bill Saunders, Sister Anne Frances/Sisters of Mercy, Robert Fields, Anna Fields White, Guerry Glover, Leize Glover Bennett, Ethel Glover Morrow, Alan Miles, Curtis Dayson, Claire Cook, Marie Wine, Marie McPherson Grant, Gretchen Stringer, Amelia Bryan and family, Libby Wallace, Stacey Draper, Catherine Wallace Seabrook, and Andrew Trenholm.

I'd also like to thank photographers Billy Rutherford, Adam Ferrell, Robert Yellin, and Steve Uzell.

Research assistance was provided by: Dr. Richard Porcher, the Avery Institute, the South Carolina Room of the Charleston County Public Library, the South Carolina Library Society, the South Carolina Historical Society, Darlene Jackson of the John's Island Branch of the Charleston County Public Library, Elizabeth H. Stringfellow, Buddy Hill, Frank Moore, Lyle E. Browning, the South Carolina Department of Transportation, Charlie Philips, Special Collections at the College of Charleston, Berkeley Electric Cooperative, John Purnell and Martha Hamilton, Jim Hayes, Grey Minshew Geissler, and other friends and family who spent time helping me.

Editing assistance was provided by my friends and family.

INTRODUCTION

No one knows exactly when the American Indians on John's Island first started growing crops, but the island's first inhabitants started a tradition of farming that has survived for centuries. Some tribes practiced communal farming, and in their culture, land, livestock, and crops belonged to everyone.

Before European explorers discovered John's Island, it was inhabited by the Cusabo, Kiawah, Stono, and Bohicket tribes. The first Spanish explorers recorded that the natives had cleared fields and were planting maize and other crops. Wildlife was abundant on John's Island, as evidenced by the abundant deerskins used in the first successful trade with the Europeans. Other wildlife included panthers, red wolves, alligators, wild boar, turkey, and a large variety of waterfowl.

Spanish explorers arrived on the Carolina coast around 1520. The Spaniards, however, didn't find the treasure of precious metals they were looking for. In the book *This Our Land*, published by the South Carolina Art Association for the South Carolina Agricultural Society in 1949, the observation is made that, "The Spaniards did not stop to think that the land in the new world could be more valuable than gold itself. Bitterly disappointed in not finding what they came after, they made but one serious attempt to colonize the Carolina coast, and gradually faded from the scene. . . . In the opinion of the [English] Lords Proprietors, agriculture would be the greatest financial asset of Carolina."

The English Lords Proprietors of Carolina received their charter from King Charles II of England in 1663. Their charter reflected the English appreciation for allotting and working the land agriculturally in a way the Spaniards could not appreciate. To the English, a sense of place in the New World meant a tie to the land, a mentality that would remain amongst the descendants of settlers for generations. John's Island was in the portion of a land grant awarded to Lord John Colleton of Barbados, from where the name St. John's is derived. The Native Americans welcomed the English settlers and showed them how to live off the Lowcountry land.

In 1666, Dr. Henry Woodward was one of the most intriguing figures in the Colonial era. Woodward was instrumental in the settlement of the state, and some historians credit him with the introduction of rice culture. Rice was originally grown in upland soil, but it was later grown in low, flooded fields tended with the skilled labor and knowledge of slaves. Dr. Woodward was granted large tracts of land and built a house on the Abbapoola Creek on John's Island.

During the Colonial period, many types of settlers came to John's Island, including Quakers, Huguenots, Scotch Presbyterians, Dutch, and Swiss. Elaborate homes like Fenwick Hall began to appear during this period. During the Revolutionary War, British commander Sir Henry Clinton made his headquarters at Fenwick, and the plantation kept the name Headquarters for over a century. Other John's Island rice and indigo plantations, such as Brick House, Bosomworth, Mullet Hall, and Peaceful Retreat, rose to prominence, but at a great cost to African American slaves. The 1790 census shows that John's Island had 600 whites, 4,660 slaves, and 40 free blacks.

After the Revolutionary War, sea-island, long-staple cotton became the primary plantation crop. It brought wealth and fame to sea-island planters and caused them to rely even more heavily upon slave labor to meet the demand. John's Island planter Kinsey Burden perfected the seed selection process and produced the most sought-after crops of sea-island cotton.

During the War Between the States, Union forces occupied Kiawah and Seabrook Island. As in the American Revolution, John's Island stood between the invaders and their prize—Charleston. The Stono Scouts fought to prevent the Union army's progress. After the war ended in 1865, the residents of John's Island returned to burned out, abandoned plantations and attempted to rebuild their agrarian economy.

The period of Reconstruction brought the first advancements for the island's newly freed African Americans. The Freedman's Bureau began land reform and schools for blacks in 1868. Black citizens built their own churches and worked to establish a sense of community for the first time as free people. The rural lifestyle on the island centered on farming and lumbering.

The 20th century brought the beginning of the end of John's Island's rural isolation when the first telephone and power lines reached the island. In the 1940s, World War II had an effect on the economy and the people. During the 1950s and 1960s, community leaders such as Septima Clark and Esau Jenkins promoted better education, voting rights, and basic human rights for African Americans, and Moving Star Hall and the Progressive Club served as centers of inspiration during those times.

In the 1970s, many farms on John's Island began large-scale commercial tomato production, which brought an influx of Hispanic workers, adding to the rich cultural diversity of the island. Though tomato farming was prosperous until the late 1980s, like many of the sea islands, John's Island drew the attention of real-estate developers, which began to have an affect upon real-estate values, retail markets, traffic, and property taxes.

John's Island is slowly losing its rural ambiance and natural beauty as more land is being developed. Today only two farmers still produce row crops commercially, while other families try to find alternative agricultural uses for their land in hopes of keeping it for future generations.

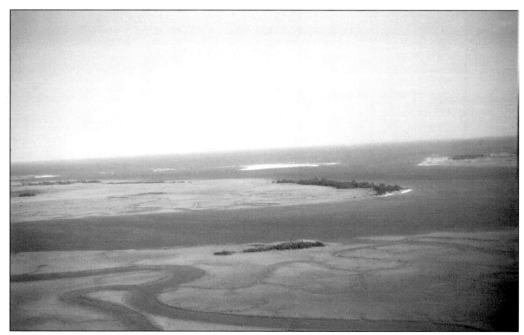

The Stono River winds around much of John's Island and meets the ocean between Kiawah Island and Bird Key. This 1950s aerial photograph looks toward the ocean from over Legareville on John's Island. (Courtesy of Jane Jenkins Herlong.)

One

THE FIRST PLANTERS

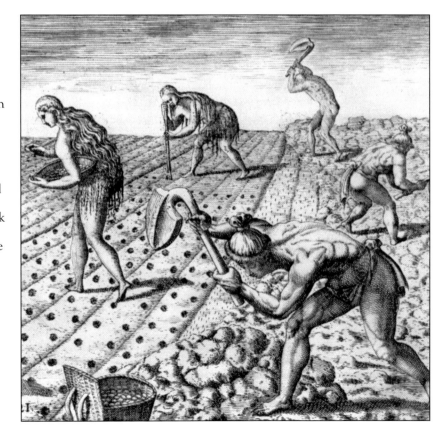

The Cusabos started a tradition of farming that has survived for centuries on John's Island. The men used crude hoes made from animal or fish bones attached to a wooden handle to break the ground and mound the furrows. The women came behind them making holes with a long stick for the corn, melon, or bean seeds. (Courtesy of *The New World*, Stefan Lorant, 1946.)

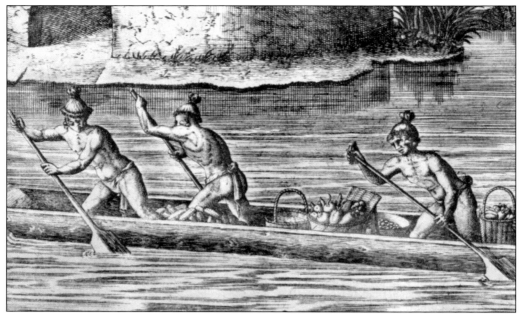

The natives made pots from clay found in creek banks and baskets woven with native grasses. When the harvest was ready, they used these to gather the food. They made long dugout canoes for fishing, traveling around the island, and transporting their produce to storage houses. (Courtesy of *The New World*, Stefan Lorant, 1946.)

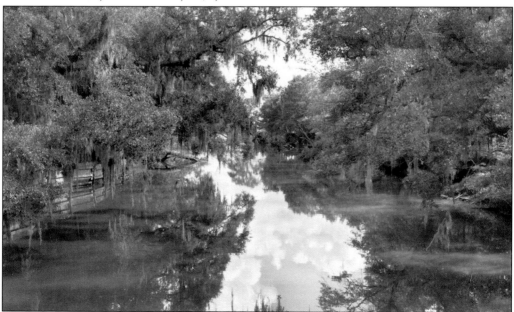

Rice and indigo were the first lucrative crops, depending heavily on the skill and labor provided by slaves imported from Barbados and other British colonies. Hundreds of slaves dug what is called Simmons Creek today (on north River Road), probably as part of a rice cultivation system. Canals and dikes created fresh water ponds for the rice. Wooden "trunks" or gates let water in or out with the tides to flood or drain the fields. (Photographer Billy Rutherford.)

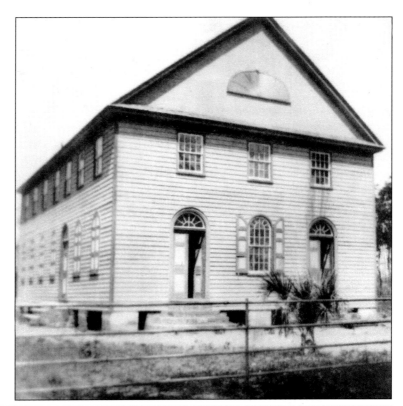

Erected in 1719, John's Island Presbyterian Church on Bohicket Road was one of the first churches to be built. The congregation was organized in 1710 under the leadership of Rev. Archibald Stobo, and services were scheduled in accordance with tidal changes. The foundation was made from bricks used as ballast in ships, and the step treads on either side of the building are covered with Italian marble. (Courtesy of Anne Grimball Minshew.)

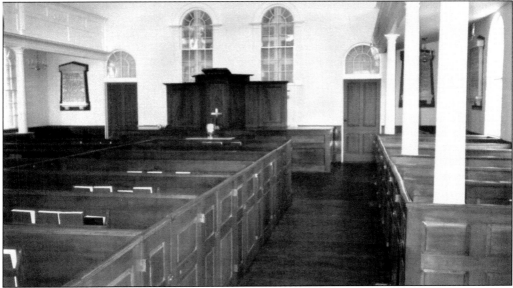

The church is one of the oldest wooden-frame churches in use in America today. In 1995, restoration work began to return the sanctuary to its original appearance. The slave galleries, added in 1823; the 9-foot-high pulpit; and colonial-style box pews have been carefully preserved. The church is on the National Register of Historic Places and offers free tours weekly to the public. (Courtesy of Mary and Billy Hills.)

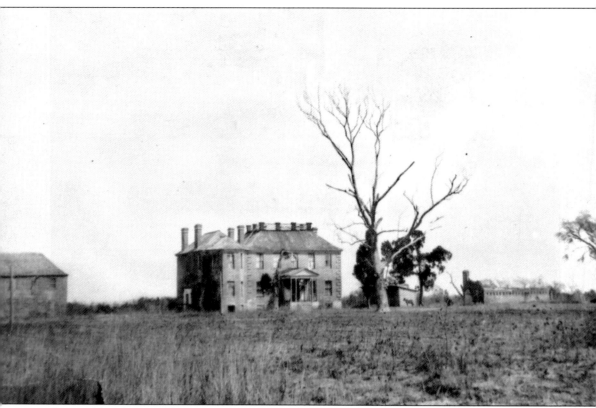

Some of the planters, like John Fenwick, were wealthy when they arrived and built elaborate homes on their new plantations. Fenwick Hall built c. 1730 off River Road, is the oldest plantation house remaining on the island. Called Headquarters for almost a century because it was occupied by troops in the American Revolution and the Civil War, it was originally part of a 3,000-acre land grant given to Gov. Robert Gibbes from the Lords Proprietors in 1702. The plantation remained in the Fenwick family for three generations and become one of the most famous horse farms in America, called the John's Island Stud. The Fenwicks also helped found the first South Carolina Jockey Club in 1758 and built a three-and-a-half-mile horse track for their thoroughbreds where Maybank Highway is today. Architectural and historic consultant Robert Stockton describes Fenwick as "an outstanding example of Palladian/Georgian domestic architecture in America and one of the best surviving 18th century country houses built by the colonial aristocracy of South Carolina." It is on the National Register of Historic Places. (Courtesy of Joe and Henry Rivers.)

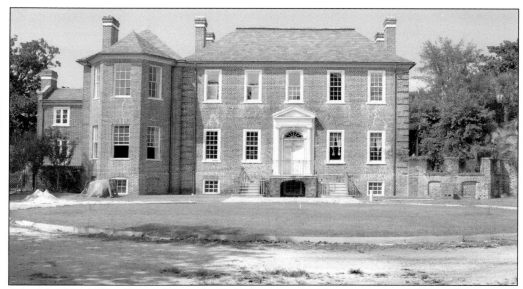

After the Civil War, Fenwick was divided, changing hands many times. Mr. and Mrs. Victor Morawetz of New York bought and restored Fenwick in the 1930s. Mr. Morawetz, a wealthy corporate lawyer, contributed generously to the community. People locally appreciated his unusual cactus garden and the beautiful avenue of magnolias he planted at the Charleston Municipal Golf Course along Maybank Highway on James Island. A new wing at Roper Hospital was named in his honor. (Photographer Billy Rutherford.)

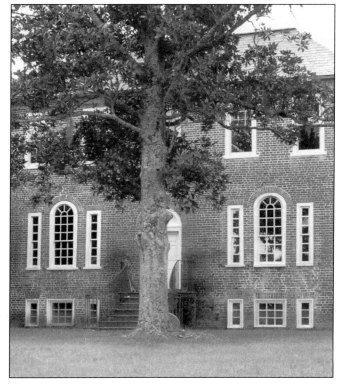

The present owners have begun a new phase of restoration work at Fenwick Hall. The roof banister seen on the left was not original and has been removed. The historic integrity of the property had already been compromised by the high-density developments built around it after the area was rezoned. The large Palladian windows on the west facade are some of the earliest of this type to be built in the Lowcountry. (Photographer Billy Rutherford.)

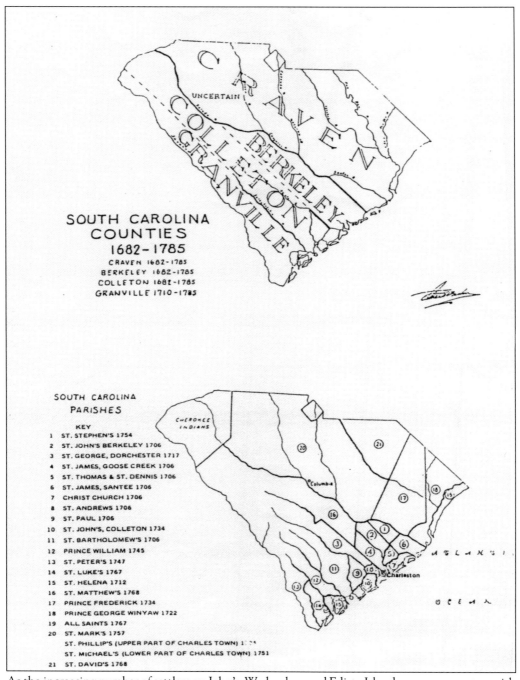

As the increasing number of settlers on John's, Wadmalaw, and Edisto Islands grew, a separate parish called St. John's, Colleton was formed in 1734. This map shows the division of the new parish.

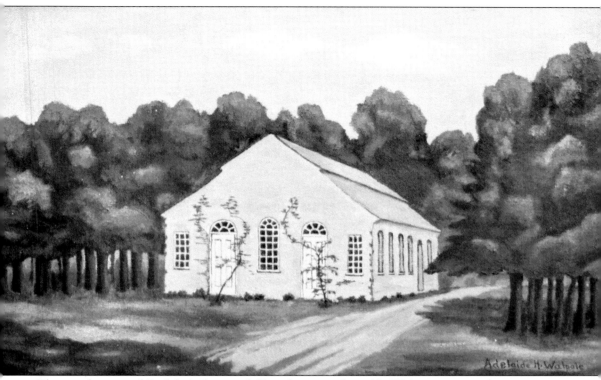

The parishioners of St. John's Episcopal Church met on June 18, 1734, to vote on a location to build a church. It was built with brick and tabby near Church Creek on land owned by Abraham Waight near the Angel Oak. The first minister, Rev. Samuel Quincey, arrived in 1742, when the church was completed. Provincial law at the time required all men going to church to carry arms because of the slave rebellion in 1739. Sadly, after the Revolutionary War and occupation by British troops, the church lay in ruins. Some of the founding members were Col. John Gibbes, John Stayarne Jr., Capt. John Jenkins, Capt. Samuel Underwood, and Thomas Hext. (Painting by Adelaide Dotterer Walpole.)

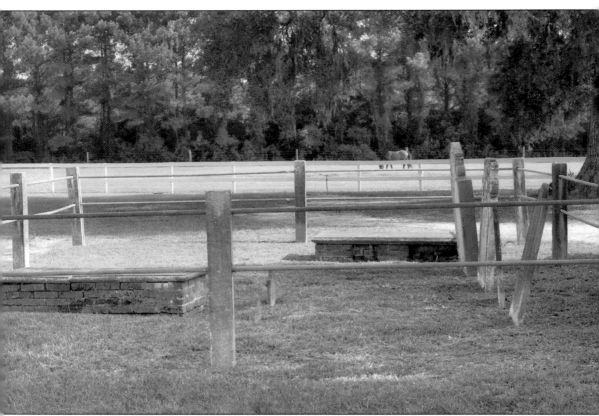

Most of the wealthy planters' homes built before the Revolution have vanished. The Stanyarne family graveyard is the only reminder of Brick House plantation off Bryan Dairy Road. The two-story Greek Revival home was built on the north side of the Abbapoola Creek and had a two-tiered, columned front porch. The Stanyarnes owned the plantation from 1696 to 1836 and grew rice and indigo. Dr. Benjamin Dart Roper and his son, Dr. William Roper, bought the plantation in 1837 and grew sea-island, long-staple cotton. It was damaged during the Civil War and suffered from years of neglect. Mrs. Morawetz of Fenwick Hall tried to help the new owner save Brick House in the 1930s, but the cost to restore the house was too great, and it was torn down in the 1950s. Mrs. Morawetz had an iron-rail fence installed around the Stanyarne family cemetery to protect it. Joseph Stanyarne Sr. (1700–1772) and other members of his family are buried here. Charleston Area Therapeutic Riding is located on Brick House today (see page 125). (Photographer Billy Rutherford.)

Though the successful planter, John Stanyarne Sr. spent most of his time at his primary residence at Brick House, but he also owned all of Kiawah Island by 1737 where he had a lucrative cattle ranch. In 1757, he became well known for one of the finest crops of indigo shipped abroad. After his death in 1772, his granddaughter Elizabeth Raven Vanderhorst and her husband, Arnoldus, began building a plantation house that was almost destroyed when British troops occupied the island during the Revolutionary War. Though pillaged a second time during the Civil War, the house remained in the Vanderhorst family until 1943. (Courtesy of Anne Grimball Minshew.)

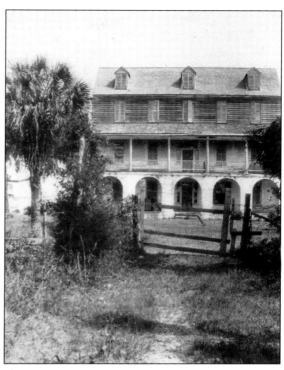

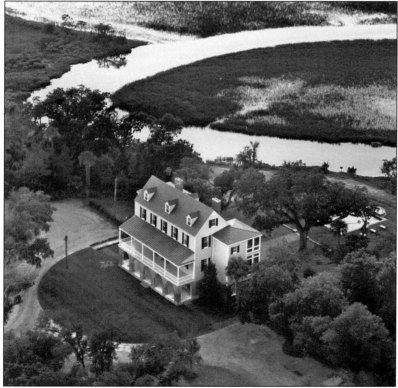

The Vanderhorst House on Kiawah was used briefly by U.S. Army beach patrols during World War II and later for hunting parties, when C. C. Royal and his wife, Eugenia, bought it in 1955. In 1994, the new owners, the Darby family, had the mansion fully and carefully restored to its original appearance. It is on the National Register of Historic Places. (Courtesy of Kiawah Real Estate Company. Photographer Steve Uzell.)

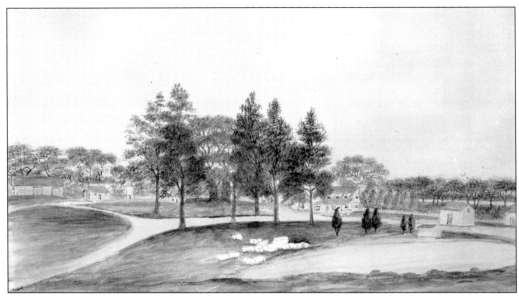

After the Revolutionary War, sea-island cotton replaced rice and indigo as John's Island's main cash crop. In their book, *The Story of Sea Island Cotton*, Dr. Richard Porcher and Sarah Fick write, "Kinsey Burden . . . played the most important role in the development of sea island cotton." His daughter, Portia B. Trenholm, painted this picture of his plantation, Oakvale, on the Stono River, where Burden perfected the process of seed selection to produce one of the finest-quality sea-island, long-staple cotton fibers ever grown. (Courtesy of Annie Caroline and George Marion Reid.)

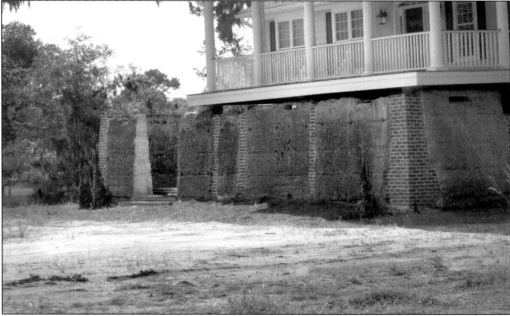

These tabby ruins off Burden Creek Road are the only visible remains of Oakvale plantation. They may have been Kinsey Burden's seed house or ruins from Robert Gibbes' plantation, Peaceful Retreat, which preceded Oakvale. The ruins have been incorporated into the foundation of a new residence in Stono Point subdivision off River Road. (Photographer Billy Rutherford.)

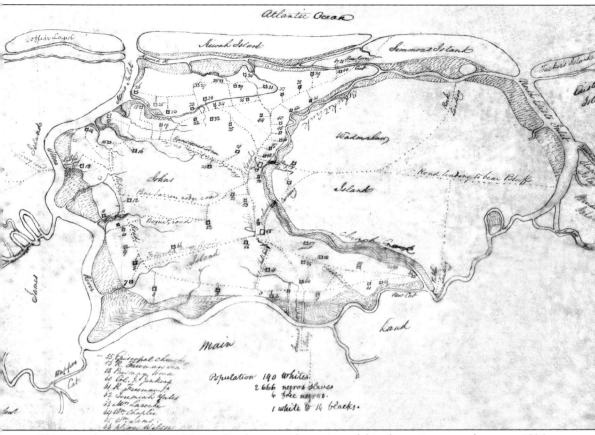

This map drawn by planter Kinsey Burden provides a view of the plantation tracts between 1826 and 1836. Though these plantations were subdivided many times after the Civil War, many of the descendants of these planters still own portions of the original lands of their ancestors. (Courtesy of Charleston Library Society, Charleston, SC.)

1. T. B. Seabrook
2. T. Simmons
3. L. L. Gibbes
4. J Moore Matthews
5. Estate Forrester
6. E. Reynolds
7. Cal I. Ward
8. Cal I. Ward
9. James Mair
10. Thomas Legare
11. Kinsey Burden
12. Micah Jenkins
13. Rev. Paul T. Gervais
14. Paul C. Grimball
15. John Dawson
16. William Backlock
17. Thomas Hanscome
18. Thomas Hanscome
19. William Whaley
20. Paul C. Grimball
21. William Robinson
22. Miss A. Stanyarne Jr.
23. Dr. H. P. Holmes
24. Mrs. B. Matthews
25. Mrs. B. Matthews
26. Edward Whaley
27. Mrs. Rush
28. Hugh Wilson
29. B. D. Roper
30. S. Witter
31. James Legare
32. Thomas Matthews
33. ? Hart
34. Thomas Legare
35. Mrs. Ball
36. James Legare
37. E. C. Fripp
38. Capt. R. Jenkins
39. John Holmes
40. William Seabrook
41. Commodore Campbell
42. Estate of Jenkins
43. Commodore Campbell
44. Capt. R. Jenkins
45. Commodore Campbell
46. Commodore Campbell
47. Mrs. Ball
48. Dr. Stevens
49. Presbyterian Church
50. Free Straphon
51. Miss A. Stanyarne Sr.
52. Micah Jenkins
53.
54. Justus Angel
55. Episcopal Church
56. B. (or R.) Freeman Sr.
57. Estate of Jenkins
58. Parsonage House
59.
60. Col. J. Jenkins
61. B. or R. Freeman Jr.
62. Jeremiah Yates
63. Wm? or Mrs. LaRoche
64. William Chaplin
65. William Sams
66. Abram Wilson
67. William Seabrook

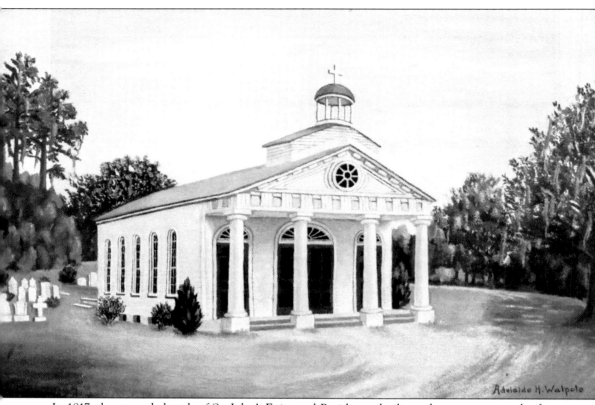

In 1817, the second church of St. John's Episcopal Parish was built on the same spot as the first. Designed by famous South Carolina architect Robert Mills, it was a simple antebellum church 45 feet long and 32 feet wide with a columned portico and a cupola. The Reverend Paul T. Gervais was the first rector to serve in the new church, and his descendants, who still live on the island, are active members of the parish. This second church was destroyed in a fire that swept through the island in 1864. The John's Island Presbyterian Church on Bohicket Road offered to share their sanctuary with them until they could build a new church. On April 27, 1873, a new church was completed and consecrated by Bishop Howe. (Painting by Adelaide H. Walpole.)

Two

THE SEEDS OF WAR

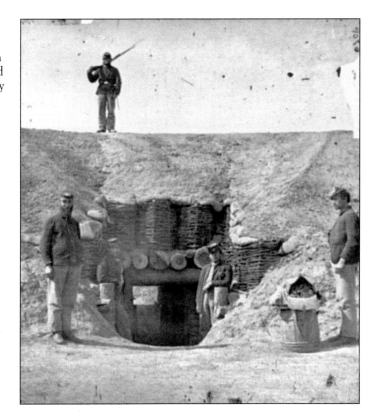

With South Carolina's secession in 1860 and the shots fired on Fort Sumter in April of 1861, war soon raged across the South. In February 1863, an order was given for civilians to evacuate James and John's Islands. To prevent the Federals from dominating the Stono River and mounting an assault on Charleston from the south, Fort Trenholm was constructed on the banks of the river. It was named for George Alfred Trenholm because of his generous contributions to its construction. These Civil War soldiers are pictured at an earthwork battery similar to the one at Fort Trenholm. A bridge to nearby Pine Island was built to move 14 to 17 heavy guns to the fort. (Courtesy of Library of Congress.)

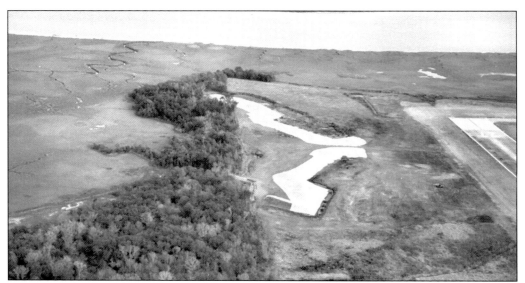

Fort Trenholm is described in the National Register of Historic Places as "the largest earthen fort in the Charleston Theatre of Operations." Hundreds of slaves and troops built the triangular, three-bastion fort on Bosomworth and Saxby plantations bordering the Stono River, seen in the background, in just six months. The highest elevation was over 27 feet on the southwest bastion, with walls 920 feet long on the northwest, 927 on the southeast, and 631 on the southwest. (Courtesy of Lyle Browning, Browning and Associates, Ltd.)

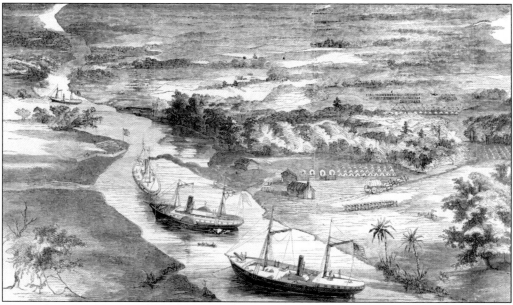

This etching by a Union soldier shows gunships in the Stono River with Fort Trenholm depicted on the left. In 1863, cannon fire from Fort Trenholm, Fort Pringle (James Island), and other batteries disabled the Union gunship *Isaac P. Smith*, causing it to become the only naval vessel in U.S. history to surrender to land-based forces. Confederate forces renamed it *Stono* and ran it aground near Fort Moultrie on Sullivan's island attempting to run the Union blockade. They burned it to prevent its recovery by the enemy. (Courtesy of Douglas W. Bostic.)

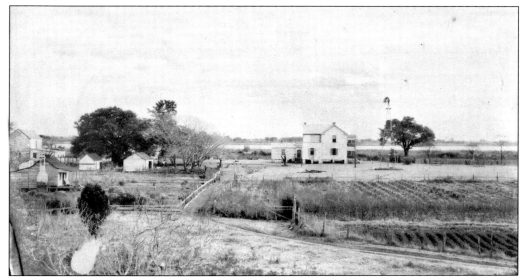

Saxby plantation off River Road was deeded to George Saxby in 1741. This picture was taken when it was owned by Paul Grimball in the 1930s. Torn down in 1943, only a cemetery remains on the site. Four of the remaining tombstones bear the names Christopher Brown, South Carolina Private, 156 Depot Brigade, August 26, 1930; Thomas Brown, September 15, 1868–January 31, 1931; Abraham Brown Jr., February 6, 1874–November 1, 1924; and Josephine Jenkins, July 25, 1898–October 10, 1939. Saxby Plantation and Bosomworth Plantation next to it bordered the Stono River and seemed the ideal location to build Fort Trenholm and other small batteries. (Courtesy of Anne Grimball Minshew.)

The Stono Scouts were an independent rifle company under the command of Capt. John Bassnet Legare Walpole. It grew from 25 planters to over 100 men who were determined to prevent Union troops from assaulting Charleston from the south. A partial roster is above.

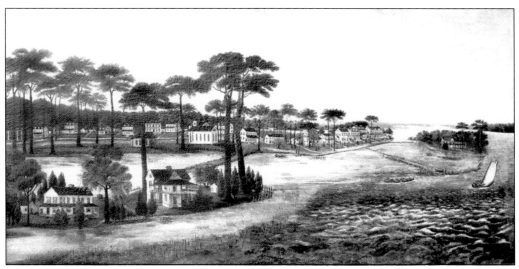

In the path of the Union army was the village of Legareville, a summer resort community between the Abbapoola Creek and the Stono River. Wealthy planters sought relief there from summer heat and mosquitoes carrying malaria. Solomon Legare set aside 10 to 12 acres for the village c. 1837.

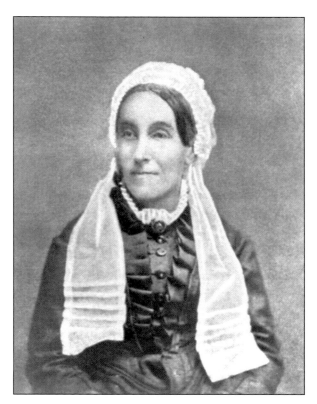

Portia Ash Burden Trenholm, daughter of Kinsey and Mary Legare Burden, painted two pictures from sketches she made of Legareville. The earliest oil painting is part of the Rockefeller Folk Art Collection in Williamsburg, Virginia. The second oil painting (seen above) is privately owned by descendants of the Burden family. Trenholm completed it c. 1870, and it is believed to be the most accurate depiction of Legareville. (Courtesy of Andrew Trenholm.)

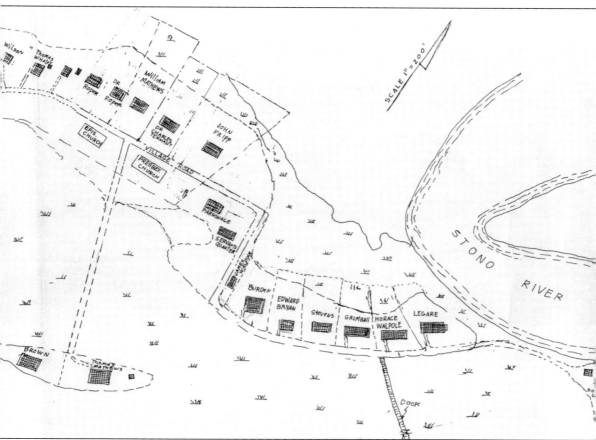

This plat by John Warren and Elizabeth W. Noble shows the families that owned summer homes at Legareville in the 1860s. According to historian Ethel Nepveux, the village, in existence for 26 years, had homes on three-quarter-acre lots, a schoolhouse, servants' quarters, chapels of ease for the St. John's Episcopal Parish and John's Island Presbyterian Church, a parsonage, and a sturdy boat landing.

John's Island, August 21, 1864

Last night at 9:00 o'clock I burnt Legareville. The buildings were at almost the same instant set on fire and were in a few minutes a sheet of flames. The battery on Horse Island fired a farewell shot into the picket house before we had left. After a considerable time the battery and gunboat renewed their fire, throwing their shell into the village and up the peninsula upon which Legareville stood to Bryan's place, a distance of three miles. Some 15 or 20 shots were fired, from which we sustained no injury. When the determination to destroy the village was announced the Stono Scouts, owners of the property on the place, volunteered to aid the detachment from Captain Clark's company ordered for the purpose, 16 such members applying the torch to their own dwellings. Today, after 16 months' duty on this outpost, I turn over the command to Captain Parker, and report to my regiment with regret that my last official act on the island should have been, under an imperative sense of duty, to recommend the destruction of the property and assisting with my own hands in applying the torch to their dwellings. I am only reconciled by the reflection that the property had served useful ends to the enemy, who were removing it for their own accomodation to the islands in their possession, and it would have been in any event lost to the owners. Five schooners, 2 brigs, and 1 gunboat in the Stono and Folly Rivers; 1 gunboat in the North Edisto River.

John Jenkins
Major, Commanding

To:
Captain H.W.Feilden
Assistant Adjutant General

The largest loss of life on the island during the war was in the Battle of Bloody Bridge (Waterloo), fought July 7–9, 1864. Gen. John P. Hatch U.S.A. landed on John's Island with over 4,000 men, marched across the island, and fought Confederates on an open field where Plow Ground and River Road meet. The small bridge crossing Burdens Creek became known as "Bloody Bridge." In August 1864, the Stono Scouts burned Legareville to prevent it from being used by Union troops who had retreated to Kiawah. This was the message written by Maj. John Jenkins of Edisto after he burned the village.

Three
Fields of Destruction

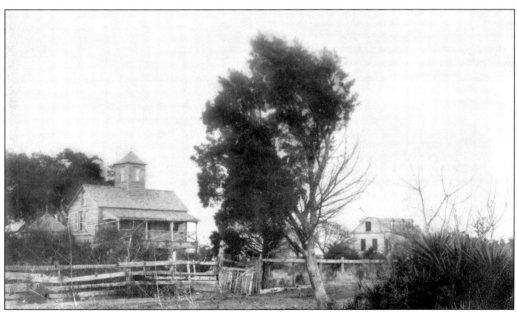

After the war, the Freedman's Bureau divided and distributed plantation land to former slaves. Planters had to rebuild simpler homes. These simple cottages were built from the ruins of Legareville after the war by family members of some of the former owners. This photograph was taken in the early 1900s, but nothing remains on the site today. The land is being carefully preserved by family descendants and not accessible to the public.

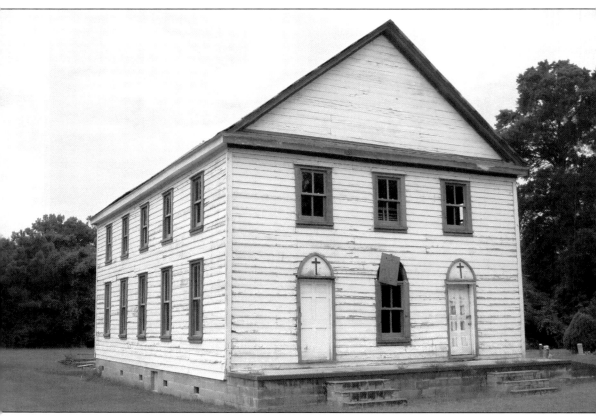

During Reconstruction, black freedmen no longer had churches to attend. They built bush tent churches made of palmetto branches and pine log poles. The Hebron Presbyterian Church is one of the oldest African American churches on John's Island. It was organized in 1865 by former slaves who had attended the John's Island Presbyterian Church up the road with their owners. They first worshipped on nearby Gregg plantation, and evangelist Ishmael Moultrie led the services. When wood from a shipwreck washed up on the beaches of Kiawah and Seabrook, they hauled it back to the church's present location on Bohicket Road and built a church patterned after their former church, John's Island Presbyterian (page 11). The architects were Jackson McGill and John Chisholm, former slaves trained as artisans on John's Island plantations. It was completed in 1870. The old sanctuary is on the National Register of Historic Places and is being restored as a senior center. (Photographer Billy Rutherford.)

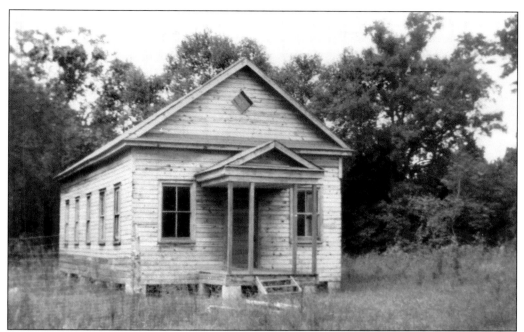

The Promiseland Church on Bohicket Road, organized c. 1865, was founded with the help of Elipha White Qualls, a white man and member of the John's Island Presbyterian Church married to a black lady named Molly. They wanted to build a place they could worship without being harassed. Renovations began in 1992 under the leadership of Rev. Bobby Taylor. It is now called Promiseland Reformed Episcopal Church. (Courtesy of Rev. Bobby Taylor.)

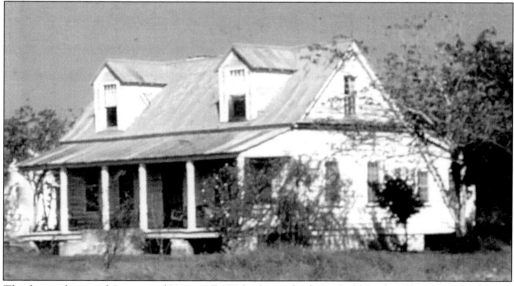

The former home of Annie and Horace E. Walpole was built on Auld Reekie Plantation built near the Abbapoola Creek in 1899 on lands formerly part of John Freer's plantation, called Edinburgh. Auld Reekie, meaning "old smoky," is the nickname for Edinburgh, Scotland. The house has been carefully preserved through the years, and the Freer family cemetery is still intact, with dates on the oldest grave 1774–1811. (Courtesy of K. Williams.)

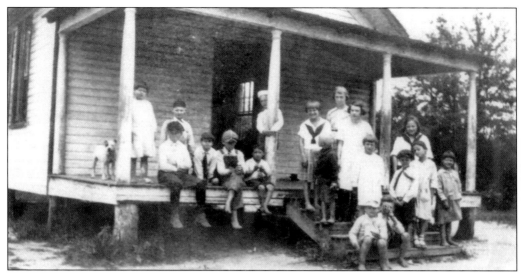

In the late 1800s, there were several small public and private schoolhouses built within walking distance of family farms. Belvidere School, attended by the Grimballs, Harts, Limehouses, and Hanahans, was built in 1898 at the intersection of Chisholm and Belvidere Roads. It was a primitive, one-room schoolhouse for first through seventh grades for 26 years until it closed in 1924, when schools consolidated. A marker was placed at the site of the former school. (Courtesy of Margaret Rivers.)

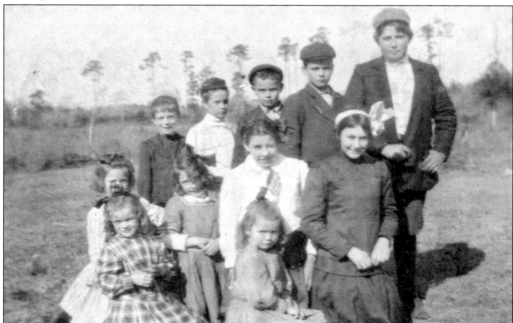

Another school was built on the south end of the island. The children in the photograph attended the Stono School in 1910. They are, from left to right, as follows: (first row) Carmen and Laura Seabrook; (second row) Rosa Walpole, Lill Legare, Lena Legare, and Beth Grimball; (third row) John Seabrook, Gene Walpole, Ben Walpole, Harold Grimball, and Ernest Grimball. (Courtesy of the Legare Family.)

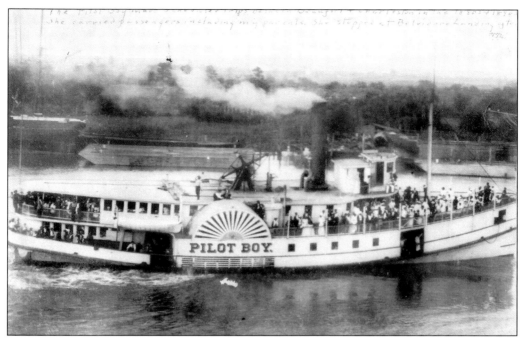

The *Pilot Boy*, piloted by Archie Jenkins of Walnut Hill, was one of the steam-driven paddle wheelers that traveled from Savannah to Charleston, picking up passengers, produce, and supplies. The *Mary Draper* and the *Lotta* were other ferries that stopped at John's Island landings in the late 1800s and early 1900s and were operated by the Stevens family. (Courtesy of Joe and Henry Rivers.)

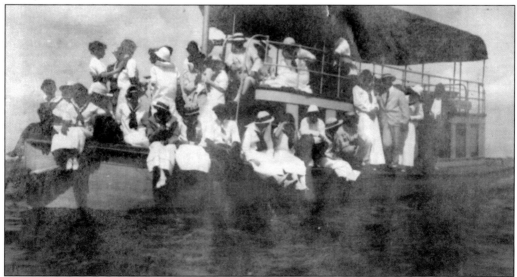

Because the schools on John's Island only went up to the seventh grade, families who could afford it sent their sons and daughters to board at Porter Military for boys or the Confederate Home for girls. They took the ferry from the island into Charleston at the beginning of the week and returned home on Friday. In 1913–1914, tuition and board at Porter Military was $300 for the year. (Courtesy of Joe and Henry Rivers.)

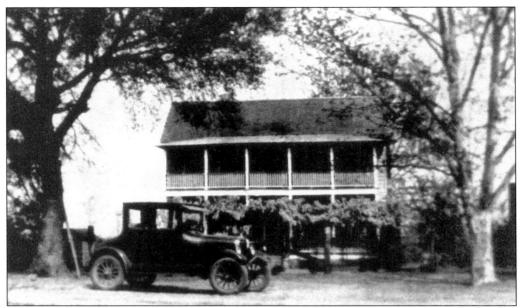

One of the oldest homes on the island is the two-story house built by John F. Limehouse in 1903 at the corner of Chisholm and Main Roads. Limehouse owned and operated the store next to his home from 1902 to 1958. He was also a farmer who operated two produce boats and brought the first car to the island on his flatbed ferry. (Courtesy of Jack Limehouse.)

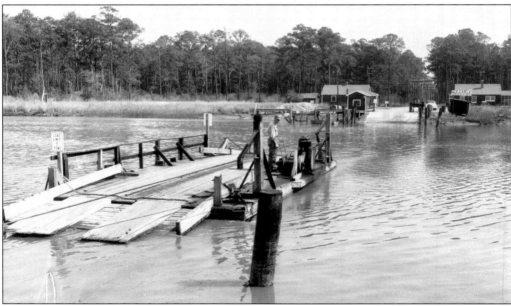

Another type of ferry that ran from the mainland to John's Island was a flatbed ferry similar to this one, pulled by cables from one side of the river to the other. When a boat needed to come through, the cables were slackened and sank to the bottom. After the ferry service went bankrupt around 1910, John F. Limehouse operated the ferry as a free service for his neighbors on the island. It operated until 1915, when the first bridge was built to the island at Main Road. (Courtesy of Charleston *Post and Courier*.)

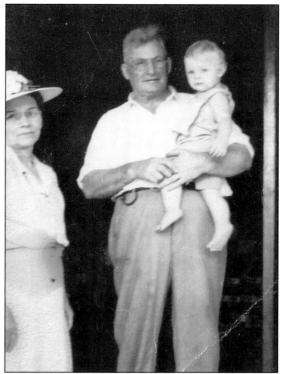

Pictured is John F. Limehouse holding his grandson John F. Limehouse II, who continued running his father's store, located at the corner of Chisholm and Main Roads, after his retirement. It was a favorite place for two generations of islanders to stop. Limehouse Sr. was famous for his pork sausage, and people came from the city and other islands just to buy it. His grandson, Jack, owner of Limehouse Produce, continues the family's reputation for selling some of the finest local produce in the Lowcountry. (Courtesy of Jack Limehouse.)

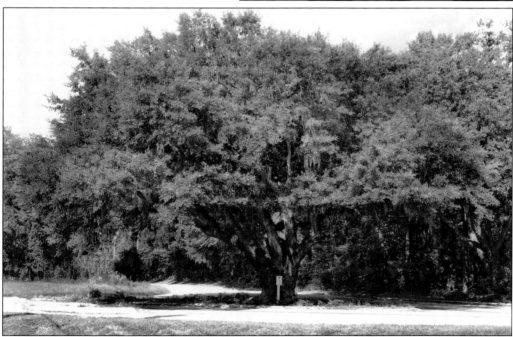

The Butcher Oak, next to Limehouse's store, was where he used to butcher his hogs and make his famous pork sausage. This plaque beside the Butcher Oak was dedicated to John F. Limehouse in 2002. (Photographer Billy Rutherford.)

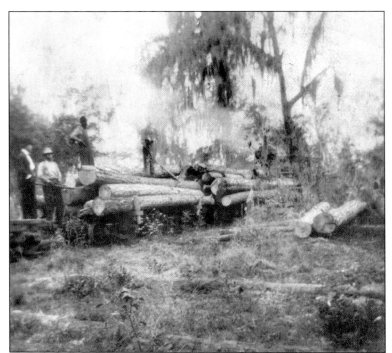

Farmers on the island commonly sold timber deeds and leases in the early 1900s to provide ready cash. Joe and Homer Eure of the North State Lumber Company, on land belonging to Thomas Legare, built a tramroad to haul timber from the Edenvale tract to Creekside plantation on the Abbapoola Creek. (Courtesy Legare and Aileen Walpole.)

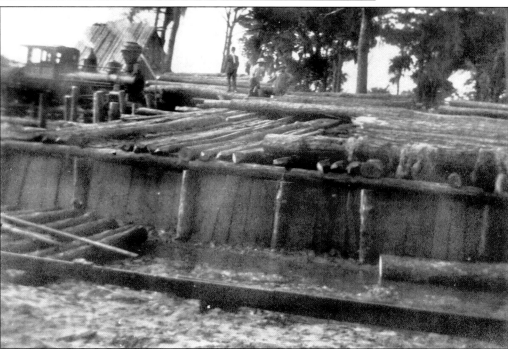

An engine pulled flatbed cars loaded with pine logs, backing down the track till it reached the river. The logs were rolled off the cars onto a log ramp and into the water at high tide. They were lashed together and rafted with the tide to the Charleston mill, where they were cut for lumber. The photograph dates to 1910. (Courtesy Legare and Aileen Walpole.)

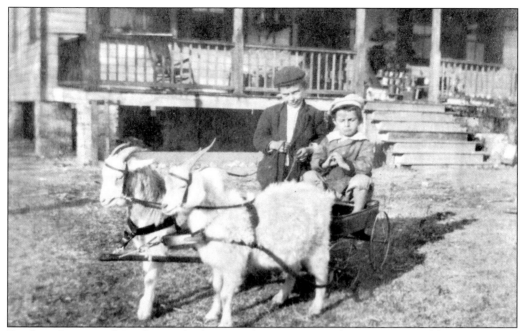

Brothers Bryan and Burden Walpole enjoyed getting around in a goat cart, like many other children on the island. They must have enjoyed watching the train unloading the logs next door to their home on Creekside plantation in 1910. The fifth generation of the family still lives on Creekside today. (Courtesy Legare and Aileen Walpole.)

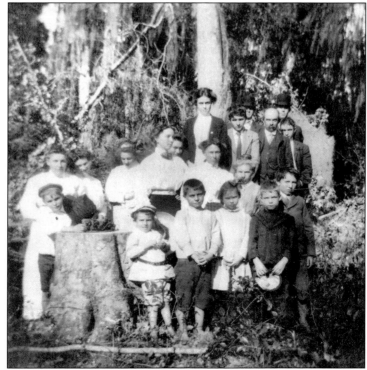

This photograph of a large family gathering is taken in the clearing where timber has been cut c. 1910. Included here are Lily Hay, Beebe Hay, Nell P. Seabrook, Rosie Hay, Belle Walpole, Hallie Reid, Dan Hay, Bassie Walpole, Nancy Hay, Siddie Walpole, John Seabrook, and Gordon Hay. (Photographs courtesy Legare and Aileen Walpole.)

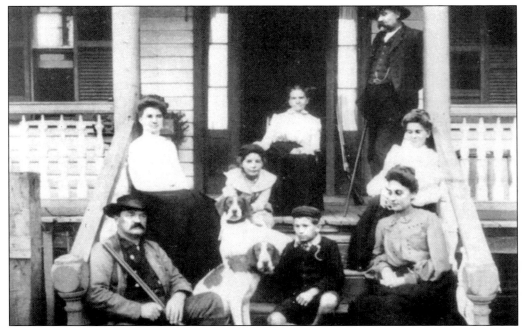

The Andell family, pictured in 1900 on the steps of their farmhouse, acquired their property in 1872. Pictured from left to right are Margaretha and William Andell on the porch and Marguerite, Marie, and Christine on the top step. Pictured with the family are Miss Saltzman, their tutor, and at front left Henry Muhler, the farm overseer who was later the postmaster at Mullet Hall. The Muhler Company of Charleston, owned by Henry Muhler Hay IV, bears his name. The boy in the front is unidentified. (Courtesy of Elizabeth Stringfellow.)

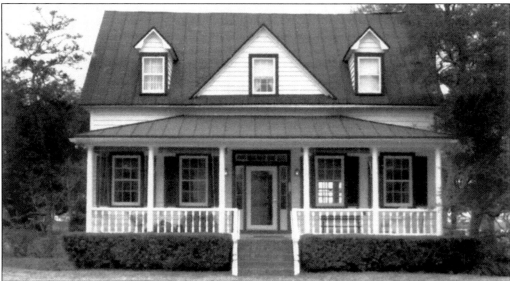

The second oldest home on the island is owned by Elizabeth Andell Hamilton Stringfellow, who authored of the book *A Place Called St. John's* restored historic Andell House, she built c. 1840. The property, off Betsy Kerrison Parkway, has been preserved with the Lowcountry Open Land Trust. (Courtesy of Elizabeth Stringfellow.)

Farming in the early 1900s was hard work. Horse-drawn plows were still being used, roads were not paved, and produce had to be delivered to markets by boat. Farmhouses like the Daniel Jenkins house at Hickory Hill, pictured here, were large but simple with no electricity or indoor plumbing. Large families were self-sufficient, growing their own crops and raising livestock. (Courtesy of Alma and Robbie LaRoche.)

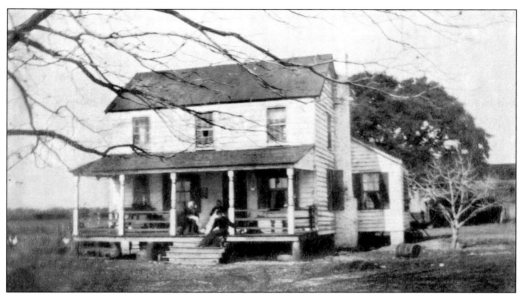

Daniel L. Jenkins, married to Elizabeth Grimball, lived at Hickory Hill off Bohicket Road and farmed Walnut Hill. He served as a magistrate on the island for 49 years, from 1914 to 1963. He held court in the Walnut Hill Schoolhouse and was well known as a tough but fair magistrate. His descendants still live on the family land at Hickory Hill and operate LaRoche Paving and Grading. (Courtesy of Alma and Robbie LaRoche.)

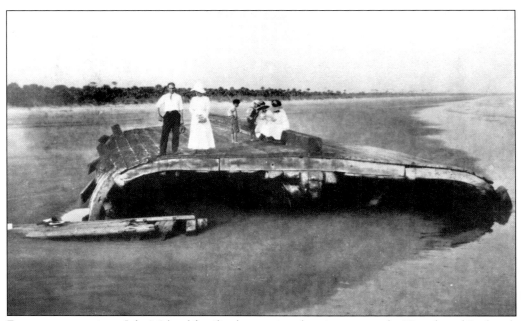

For many generations, John's Island families have enjoyed outings on nearby Kiawah and Seabrook beaches called barrier islands because they buffer sea islands or the mainland from the sea. A group poses for a picture in 1911 on the shipwrecked *Margaret A. May*, which washed up on Kiawah after a major storm. (Courtesy of John and Teddy Walpole.)

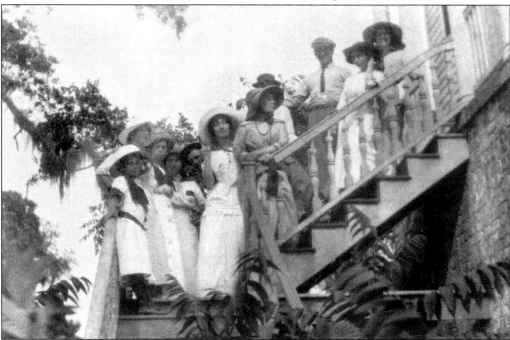

The Vanderhorst family had a large boat landing used for shipping on the Kiawah River. Many of their visitors also arrived by boat to enjoy a day at the beach. This photograph taken in 1912 shows friends gathered on the steps of the Vanderhorst house. (Courtesy of John and Teddy Walpole.)

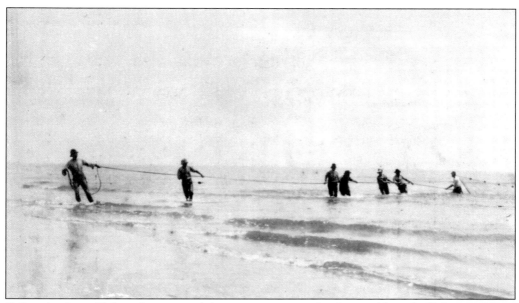

Before the days of fishing licenses and shrimping permits, islanders could catch all they could eat. It was common to see men pulling seine nets in the surf or the tidal creeks. A seine was a large net made with weights at the bottom and floats across the top. It took several people to pull the net in when filled with fish, crabs, and shrimp. This photograph was taken in 1910 at Kiawah. (Courtesy of Anne G. Minshew.)

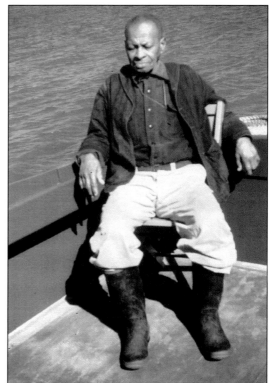

Charlie Scott lived on Kiawah all his life. He was the caretaker for the island after the last Vanderhorst family member owned the island. He had a small house and farm on the back side of the island and raised calves and pigs, which he sent to market by boat. When he wasn't farming, he was fishing. His descendants still live on John's Island. (Courtesy of Elanor Jenkins.)

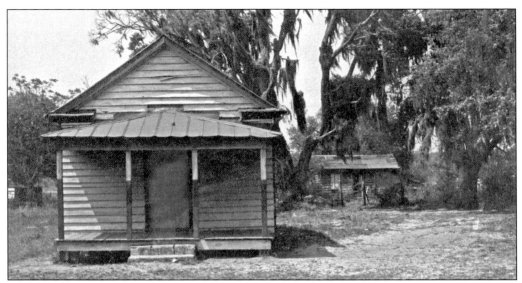

Moving Star Hall, built in 1910, is the only praise house left on the island. The black community held meetings there three nights per week in addition to Sundays for preaching, singing, shouting, and clapping to rhythms that represented the mood of worship. The beautiful songs were passed from one generation to the next. The Moving Star Society was formed to help families who didn't have enough money to pay bills, and it provided food, care for the sick, and funeral arrangements for the deceased. (Courtesy of South Carolina Room, Charleston County Public Library.)

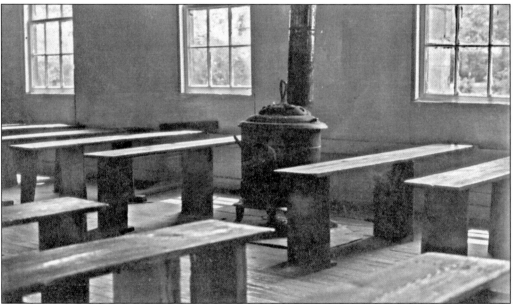

Moving Star Hall had simple wooden benches, a pot-bellied stove for heat, and a small table used for a pulpit where anyone could preach or give a testimony. It was recently remodeled, and Pastor Kay Colleton presently leads weekly Bible study meetings there. Moving Star Hall is located one mile southwest of Charleston Executive Airport on South River Road and is listed on the National Register of Historic Places. (Courtesy of South Carolina Room, Charleston County Public Library.)

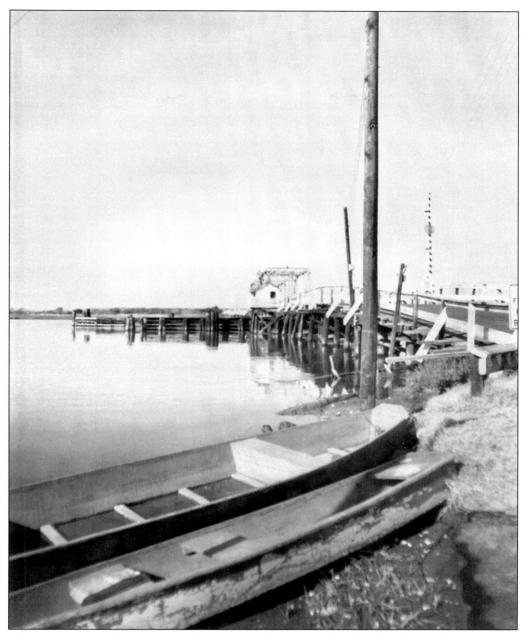
Change came c. 1917 when the John's Island bridge linked the island to the mainland at Main Road. It was a creosote wooden swing bridge with a bridge tender's house on one side. Many islanders have memories of its "clackity clack" sound as their cars passed over its wooden planks. Automobiles and trucks quickly replaced ferries as the primary means of transportation from the island. (Courtesy of Nancy Limehouse Carter.)

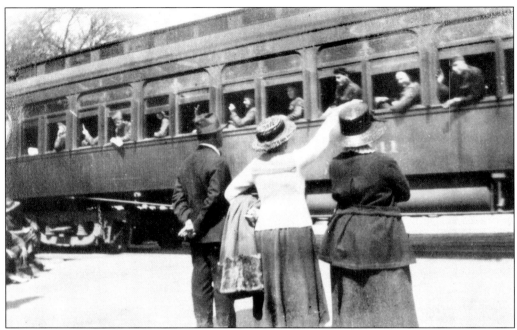

Since the 1800s, the Atlantic Coast Line Railroad (ACL) served John's Island from the mainland, where the depot was located off Main Road at Shell Point. ACL trains carried passengers, mail, and freight up and down the eastern U.S. coast. Soldiers are seen here being transported during World War I on the ACL. (Courtesy of Joe and Henry Rivers.)

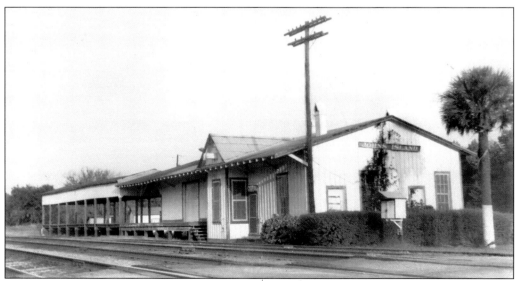

John's Island residents had to cross the Stono River to pick up their mail or freight delivered by train. The depot at Shell Point operated until the late 1960s and was later torn down, but the tracks are still in use today. (Courtesy of Frank Moore.)

Four

THE HARDSCRABBLE YEARS

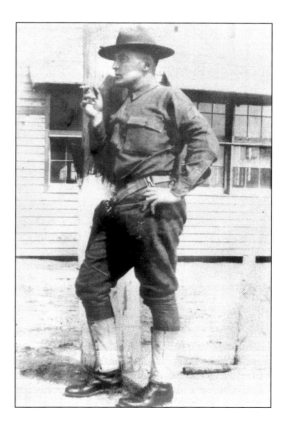

When World War I began, many islanders answered the call to defend their country. Ernest Wilkinson Grimball Sr. (August 29, 1896–March 20, 1971), the son of Frances Elizabeth Legare Grimball and Robert M. Grimball, lived on John's Island all his life. He was a cavalry sergeant in the U.S. Army in World War I and in 1918 married Frances Evans Wilson. Prior to enlisting in the army, he was a captain at Bailey Steamboat Company of Charleston. He farmed on John's Island during the 1920s and 1930s and later became a South Carolina game warden, a position he held until the 1960s. (Courtesy of Anne Grimball Minshew.)

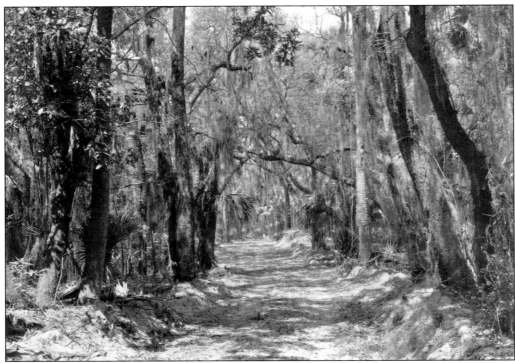

Seabrook's Beach (now Seabrook Island) was owned and farmed by the Jenkins family during World War I. As shown in the picture, the sandy roads looked quite wild and jungle-like in previous times.

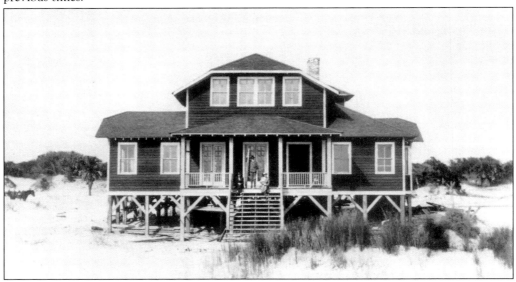

The Kiawato Clubhouse, later referred to as the clubhouse, was built for the Kiawato Hunting Club, organized in 1916 by Herman G. Leiding and others from Charleston. The two-story house on Seabrook's beach was constructed of heart pine and cypress posts and beams. It was solidly built, surviving several major storms and hurricanes. The Seabrook Island Company tore it down in 1981 to make room for new condominiums at Pelican Watch. (Courtesy of Elizabeth Stringfellow.)

Lena Legare poses on her new Chevrolet at Seabrook's Beach. Islanders brought their cars to Seabrook to drive and sometimes race on the hard-packed beach. The beach was enjoyed by many families for camping, fishing, and church youth outings. This photograph was taken in the early 1900s. (Courtesy of the Legare family.)

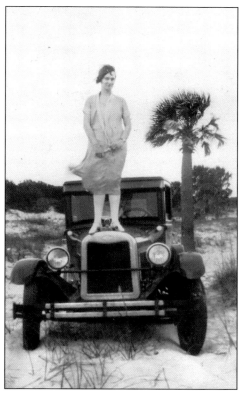

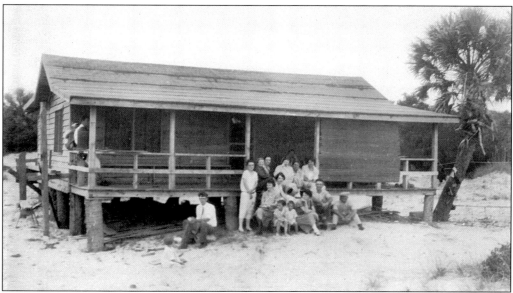

There were several old beach shacks at Seabrook, owned at different times by the Jenkins, Seabrook, and Andell families. They allowed family and friends to use these beach houses free of charge. Of course, there was no indoor plumbing or electricity, and there were a few mice to contend with. Lack of accommodations did not discourage the Legare family, seen here, from enjoying a stay at the beach. (Courtesy of the Legare family.)

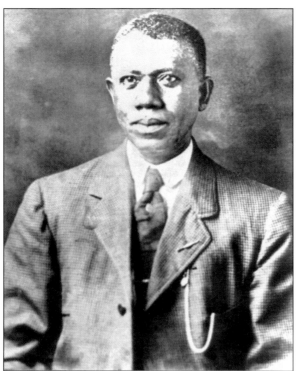

The first post office built on the island was on Main Road, where the Stono Café is today. Adam Cecil Dayson Sr. (1866–1940), John's Island's first black postmaster, served from 1892 until 1940. A graduate of Penn School in Beaufort, South Carolina, he moved to John's Island as a schoolteacher in 1885. As postmaster, he made $16 per month, which was later raised to $110 per month. He was commended at his retirement for keeping his accounts accurate and giving customers excellent service for 48 years. He was also a farmer, and he and his wife raised 11 children. Many of his descendants still live near the site of the old post office. (Courtesy of Curtis Dayson.)

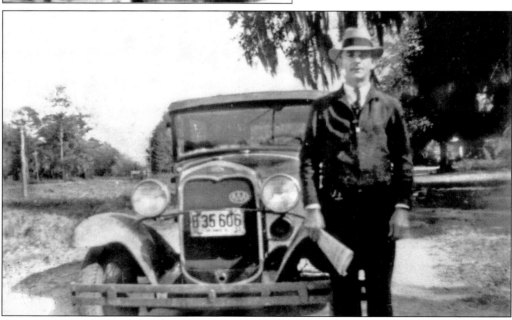

Island native and World War I veteran Clarence J. Glover served as a mail carrier under Dayson for 37 years. Starting in 1920, before roads were paved, he tried delivering mail in his Model T brass-head Ford, but found a horse and buggy more dependable for the ever-changing conditions of the rural dirt roads. He always stopped to help his postal patrons read or write their letters. His wife, Ruby, was a favorite teacher at St. John's School for 26 years. (Courtesy of Claire Cook.)

David T. Gatch was the tender for the train trestle called Stono 1 off River Road. After Seaboard Air Line Railroad built bridges to John's Island c. 1925, Gatch was responsible for opening the Stono Bridge for boats, which required the strength of two men to manually crank the cogs. Before opening the bridge, the tender climbed a pole to hang a red-shaded oil lamp at the top that signaled approaching trains to stop for the open bridge. His daughter, Elizabeth Blitch, still lives on his property on the Stono River next to where the trestle was. (Courtesy of Elizabeth Gatch Blitch.)

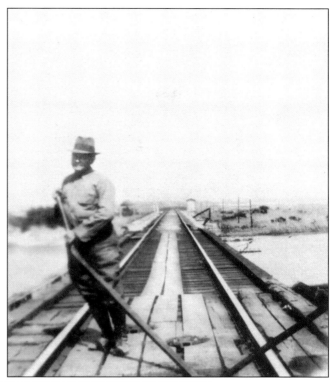

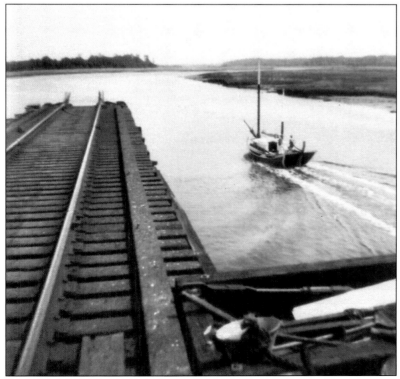

The Stono 2 train bridge was tended by Guy Leonard Buckner Sr., who worked for the Seaboard Air Line Railroad, also known as the "EC" for East Carolina route, from 1928 until 1956. The route was discontinued in 1966 and the bridges were dismantled c. 1967. (Courtesy of Doris Fowler Hardy.)

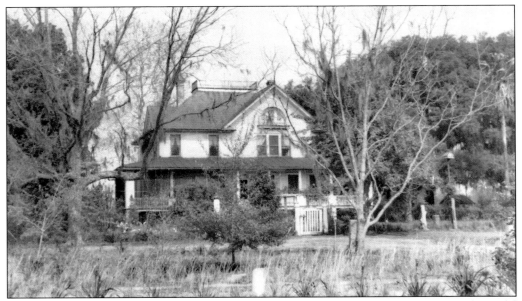

Another early-20th-century home that has been carefully preserved is Belvidere, meaning "beautiful view," the home Joseph Seabrook Hart built c. 1903 on Chisholm Road (formerly Ferry Road). He grew sea-island cotton, cabbage, and other crops. Belvidere, like many farms at that time, had a cotton gin, a commissary where tools and supplies were sold, and living quarters for employees. (Courtesy of Joe and Henry Rivers.)

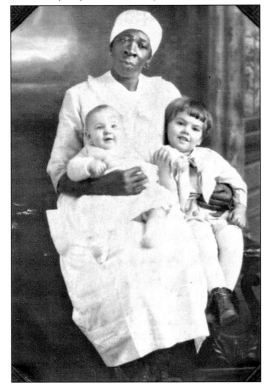

Joseph Hart sold Belvidere to his son-in-law, Henry Fowles Rivers Sr., who married Hart's daughter, Evelyn L. Hart (page 50). In this photograph, "Maum Bet" (Rebecca Heyward) is holding the Rivers children, Henry, age 1, and Joseph, at 3 (on the right). "Maum" is a French word meaning nurse or one who cares for children. Rebecca Heyward also raised three children of her own. Henry Rivers and his wife, Carmen, live at Belvidere today, and have preserved the property from development through the Lowcountry Open Land Trust. (Courtesy of Joe and Henry Rivers.)

After the boll weevil put an end to the lucrative sea island cotton crop in 1920, farmers turned to vegetable crops. Joseph Seabrook Hart Jr. (seen on the right) is standing with his grandson, Joseph LaRoche Rivers, in one of his cabbage fields at Belvidere about 1926. Cabbage became a major crop on John's Island during this time. (Courtesy of Joe and Henry Rivers.)

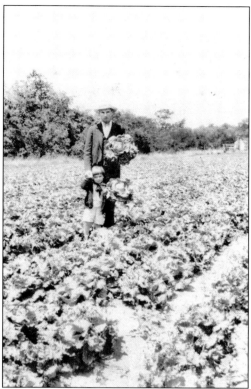

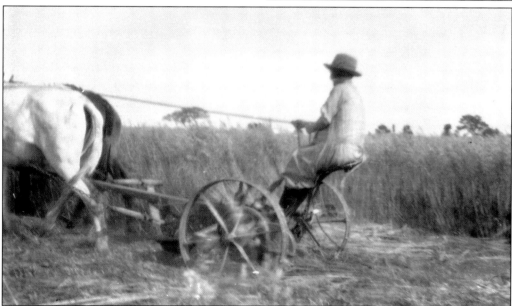

Taken in the 1920s, this photograph shows how primitive farm equipment was during this time. A mule-drawn mowing machine with a sickle bar was used to cut and clear a field before planting. Many farms had their own shops where they built many of their own implements. (Courtesy of June Walpole Dickerson.)

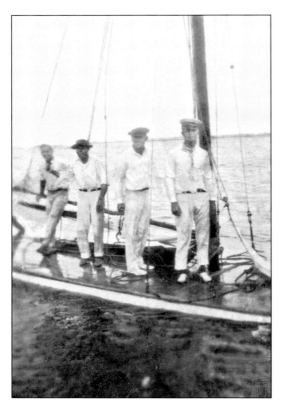

Balancing farm work with fun, John's Island families have participated in the Rockville Regatta since the 1800s. Islands formed yacht clubs and entered their boats. John's Island Yacht Club's first entrant was Manly Sullivan's swallow *Springboard*, which he gave to Ben and Genie (Eugene H. Sr.) Walpole when he built a new boat. Pictured on the boat in 1924 are crewmen Ben Walpole, Johnny Andell, George Andell, and Genie Walpole.

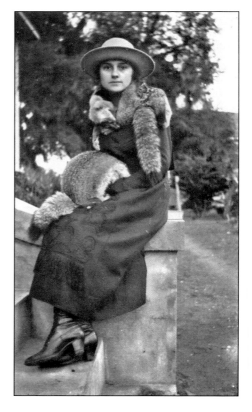

The sailboat *Springboard* was renamed *Evelyn* in honor of Evelyn LaRoche Hart of Belvidere, who is pictured at right. Her father, Joseph Seabrook Hart, was commodore of the John's Island Yacht Club at that time. (Courtesy of Joe and Henry Rivers.)

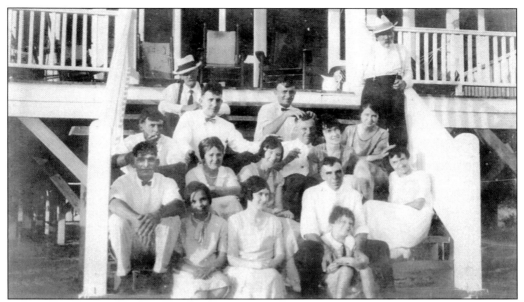

Pictured above are friends and family who gathered to watch the Rockville races. Within the group are Nancy Hay, Lena Legare, Sol Hay, Christine Andell, Rosie Hay, Vardell Legare, Johnny Andell, Thomas Legare, and George Andell. Dress for the races was casual, but a formal dance was held in the clubhouse at the conclusion of the competition. (Courtesy of the Legare family.)

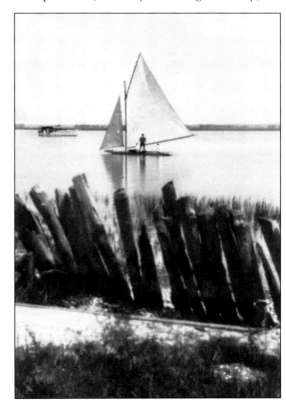

The *Evelyn*, which enjoyed much success in the Rockville Regatta in the 1920s and 1930s, is seen here under full sail. It was gaff-rigged and built on Shem Creek in Mount Pleasant around 1910. The spar seen on top of the mainsail is now on display in the Sea Island Yacht Club at Rockville. (Photograph from the collection of Cornelia Procher Walpole.)

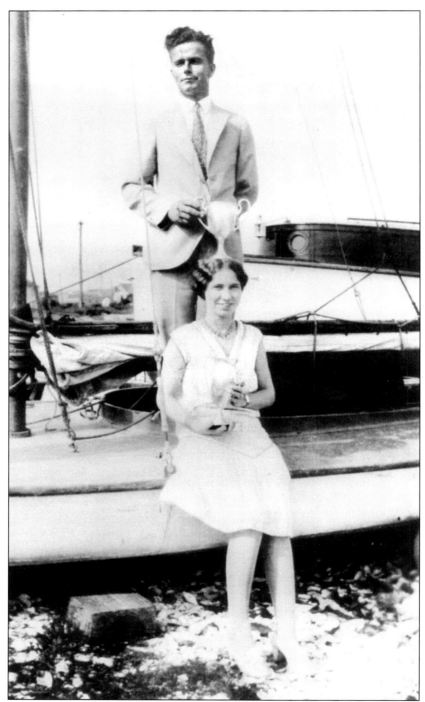

John's Island native and farmer Ben Walpole holds the Enterprise Cup he, and his crew won at Rockville three years in a row. From 1911 until 1931, Enterprise Bank sponsored the winner's trophy for the Rockville Regatta. Pictured with Ben is his future wife, Adelaide Dotterer Hill. Their son, Ben Walpole Jr., still has the Enterprise Cup. (Courtesy of Ben and Lisa Walpole.)

Country stores stocked everything necessary for life on the island. One of the prettiest country stores on the island was Howell's, at the corner of River Road and Edenvale. William Sidney Howell and his family lived above the store in his large two-story home with a second-story porch, built c. 1920. (Courtesy of Rene Saunders.)

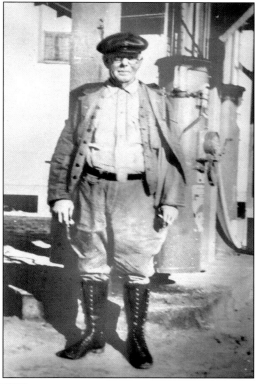

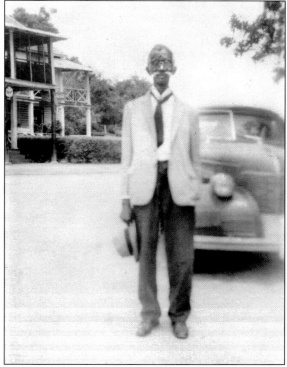

Howell also had a small sawmill and a gristmill where he ground cornmeal for his customers. His granddaughter, Lovetta Coleman Sigety, remembers he had a wall telephone in the store. When she asked him why it didn't work, he said it was because there was no service yet, but he wanted to be ready when service came available. The store burned down in the 1960s. A frequent customer, Emanuel Lee of River Road stands in front of Howell's Store.

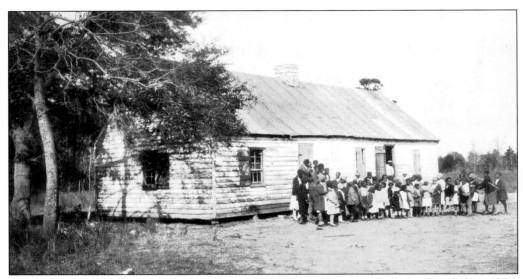

The Promise Land School was a primitive, two-room schoolhouse on Bohicket Road. One of the teachers, Septima Clark, became a civil rights leader and helped start the citizenship schools. Blacks were not allowed to teach in Charleston until the 1920s, so they came to rural areas and boarded with families who lived near the schools. Schools were painted with black creosote, to preserve the wood and a fireplace was used for heating. There were outdoor privies and a pitcher pump for water. (Courtesy of Charleston County Public Schools Department of Archives.)

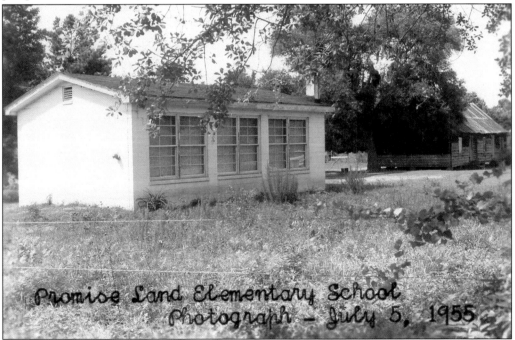

This cinder-block classroom was added behind Promiseland School at a later date. It is presently part of the Chez Fish restaurant on Betsy Kerrison Parkway. The first wooden building, seen in the background, burned down. (Courtesy of Charleston County Public Schools Department of Archives.)

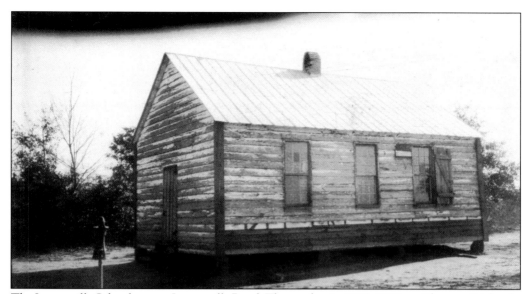

The Legareville School was on Legareville Road. The teacher in 1926–1927 was Florence Richards. The school was a Rosenwald School, one of more than 5,300 schools for black children in rural communities across the South funded by the generosity of Sears, Roebuck, and Company president Julius Rosenwald. All Rosenwald schools were painted dark green. (Courtesy of Charleston County Public Schools Department of Archives.)

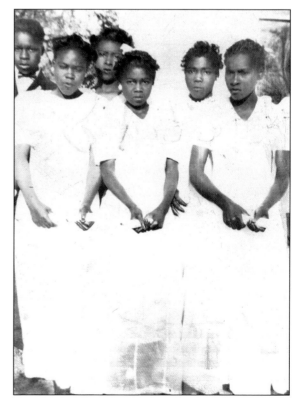

Until the 1950s, the black schools on the island taught classes through the seventh grade. Bill Jenkins, son of Esau Jenkins, remembers his father buying a bus for families who could afford to send their children to Burke School in the city of Charleston. If they couldn't go to Burke, they went to work on farms and some took night classes from tutors. Seen here is a graduating class from the Legareville School holding their diplomas. Included are Benjamin Birch, Bessie Washington, unidentified, Buella Fludd, and Isabel Smalls. (Courtesy of Avery Institute.)

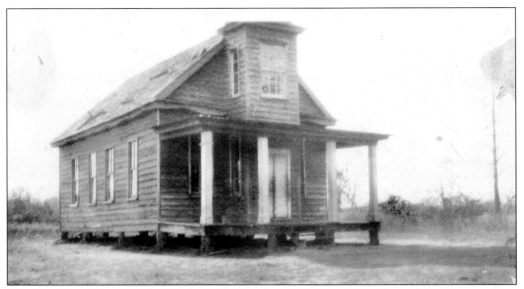

The first Haut Gap (meaning "high gap") School was built near Plow Ground Road, near where the present school stands today. The teacher at Haut Gap in 1926–1927 was Ida Zimmerman. (Courtesy of Charleston County Public Schools Department of Archives.)

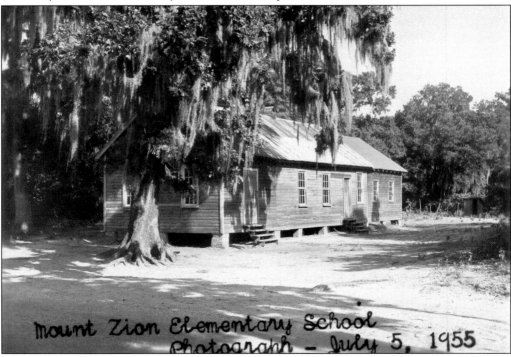

Mount Zion Elementary was formerly a one-room schoolhouse for white children called Stono School (page 30). It was built on River Road, where the old Progressive Club is today. Janie Burgess was the teacher in 1926–1927. It was later used as the first citizenship school and eventually as the Progressive Club, which was a cooperative buying club. (Courtesy of Charleston County Public Schools Department of Archives.)

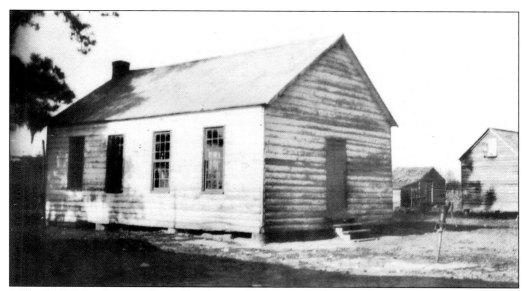

Miller Hill School was on River Road near the airport. Lydia Mikell taught there in 1926–1927. After the school closed, someone converted it into a home, which still stands today. (Courtesy of Charleston County Public Schools Department of Archives.)

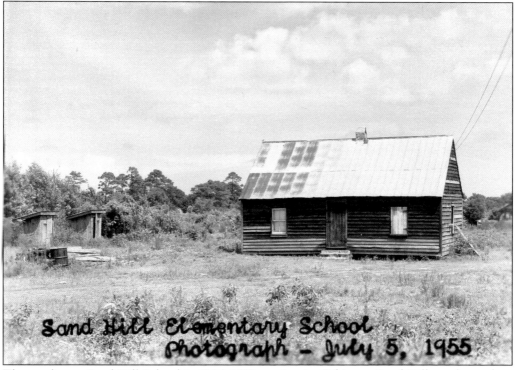

The teacher at Sand Hill School in 1926–1927 was Louise Whitney. Sand Hill was located on Bohicket Road property of William Wilson and was also a Rosenwald School. This photograph taken in 1955 shows the type of outdoor privies (at left) all the schools had in those days. (Courtesy of Charleston County Public Schools Department of Archives.)

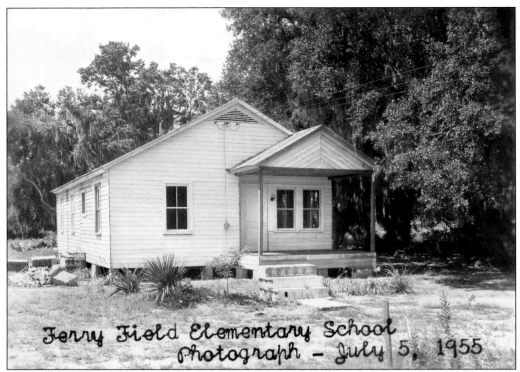

Ferry Field School was named for the Baptist church (once called "the barefoot church") at Ferry Field on North River Road. The teacher in 1926–1927 was J. R. Pearson. The school was completely renovated as a beautiful private residence, shown below. (Above, courtesy of Charleston County Public Schools Department of Archives.) (Below, photographer Billy Rutherford.)

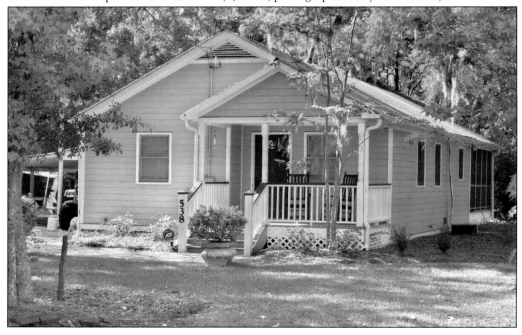

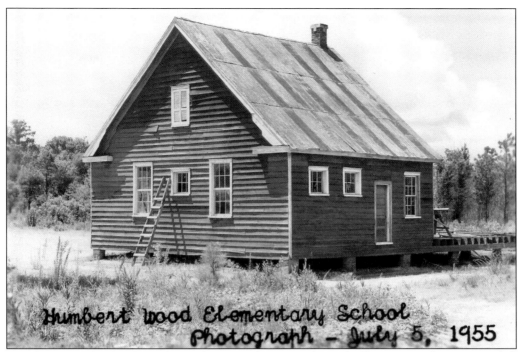

Humbert Wood School was located on Humbert Wood Road off Main Road. A. E. Tindall and Eva Campbell taught there in the 1920s. (Courtesy of Charleston County Public Schools Department of Archives.)

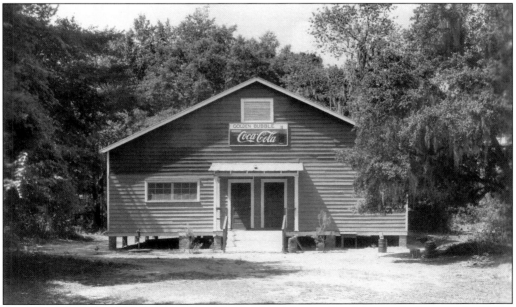

Wellington School was located on North River Road. Laura Coackley taught here in the 1920s. When black schools consolidated, it became the Golden Bubble store, where many people remember attending dances as well as May Day ceremonies for their school. It has been converted into a residence. (Courtesy of Charleston County Public Schools Department of Archives.)

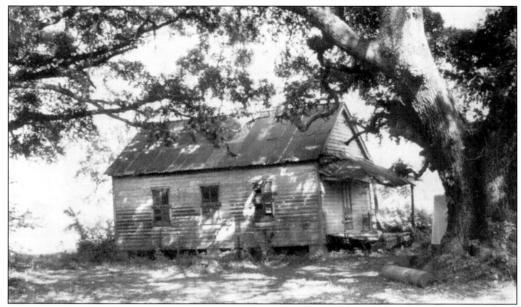

The old Walnut School on Bohicket Road was also used as a magistrate's court. It was scheduled to be torn down in the 1990s, but Betty H. Stringfellow of Andell's Bluff convinced the county to let her to move it to her property at Rosebank Farm. It is now Walnut School Museum, displaying Native American artifacts, items from the Revolutionary and Civil Wars, and relics from Mullet Hall plantation. (Courtesy Elizabeth Stringfellow.)

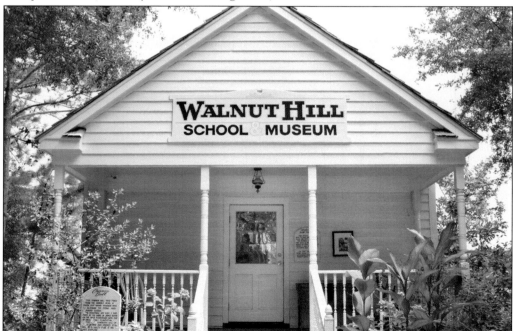

The old schoolhouse museum is open to the public at Rosebank Market off the Betsy Kerrison Parkway near the entrances to Kiawah and Seabrook. Admission is free. (Photographer Billy Rutherford.)

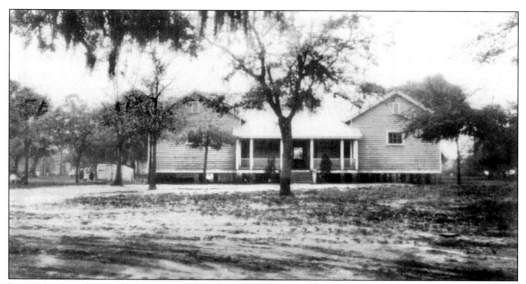

In 1923, the white schools consolidated, and St. John's School opened for grades 1 through 12. It was a multi-winged wooden structure with a porch built on 22 acres on Main Road. D. H. Marchant was the first principal. The only high school option for black students was Burke High School in Charleston until the 1950s.

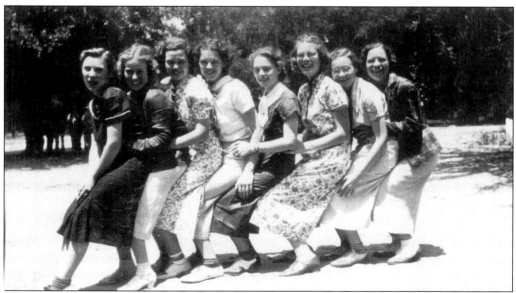

Classmates seen here at St. John's School from left to right were: Mary Williams, Greggie Seabrook, Ada Seabrook, Mary Beckett, Dimpy Limehouse, Mary Frances Michael, Alma Jenkins, and Betty Hamilton. (Courtesy of Ethel Seabrook Nevpeaux.)

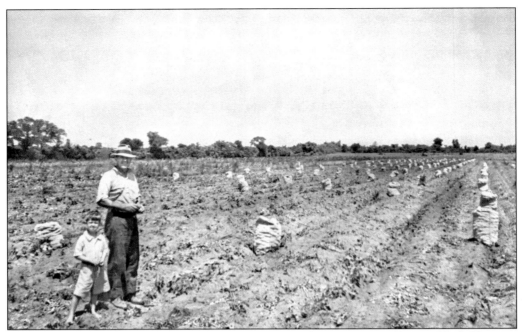

In the 1920s and 1930s, potatoes became a major crop in the Lowcountry. Eugene Vardell Legare, pictured here with son Tommy, had one of the largest potato farms on John's Island. It was located along the shores of the Stono River at the site of Hanscombe Point, which has been in Legare family since Solomon Legare first acquired it in 1725. (Courtesy of the Legare family.)

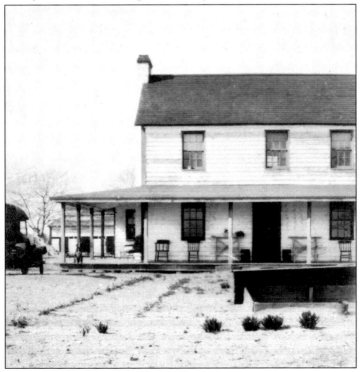

The Legare home still stands at Hanscombe Point on the Stono River. It replaced the original plantation house, which was destroyed by Union cannon fire from gunships that came up the Stono River. Tommy Legare's wife, Anne, and their children Linda, Helen, and Thomas, continue to run the family business and farm (page 120). (Courtesy of the Legare family.)

Farmer George Walter Hills produced potatoes on his 103 acres of the former Angel plantation, which he bought in 1908 for $750. The house site on Church Creek sat just across the road from the famous Angel Oak. The house pictured was built to replace the original home destroyed by the 1911 hurricane. Hills was one of the last to plant sea-island cotton when the boll weevil came through, and subsequently turned to planting Irish potatoes. (Courtesy of Bill and Mary Hills.)

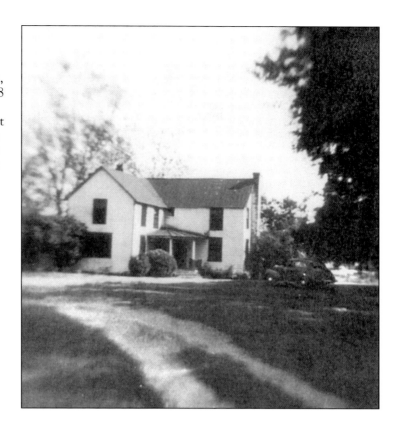

This 1934 tax receipt from Charleston County is almost unbelievable compared to the property taxes on the same waterfront property today, which is still owned by the Hills family. They converted the farm to Three Oaks nursery, the oldest nursery on the island. The family has preserved their land with the Lowcountry Open Land Trust.

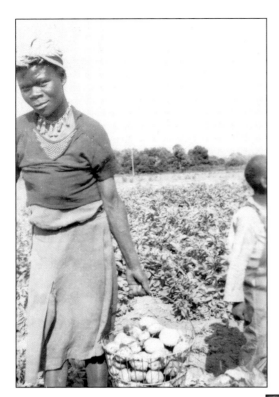

Virginia "Micey" Ramsey is shown here gathering Irish potatoes from the field on Sunnyside Farms. The potatoes were harvested in June, when school was out, so many children accompanied their parents to the fields.

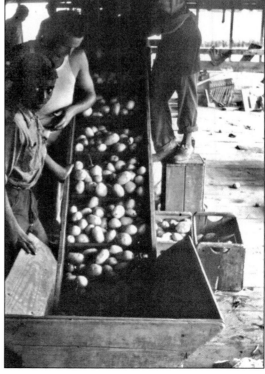

After the potato digger uprooted the potatoes, they were stacked in piles on top of the rows. They were carried to a grader, where they were sorted, packed in barrels, then covered with burlap tops secured with a metal band. (Courtesy of Eleanor Jenkins.)

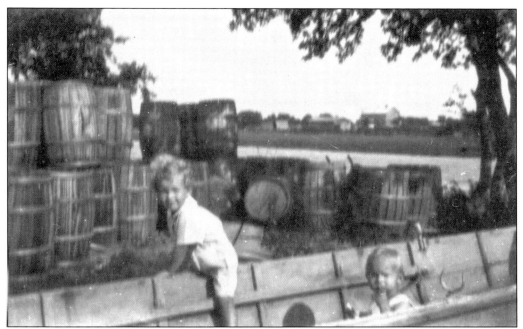

Farms bordering deep-water rivers shipped their potatoes to Charleston by boat. June and Gene (left) Walpole Jr., of Sunnyside Farms, are seen playing in front of potato barrels waiting to be picked up on the Abbapoola Creek in 1930. On the riverbanks, children made large slingshots between trees and used rejected potatoes for ammunition against friends on the other side of the river. Nothing was wasted.

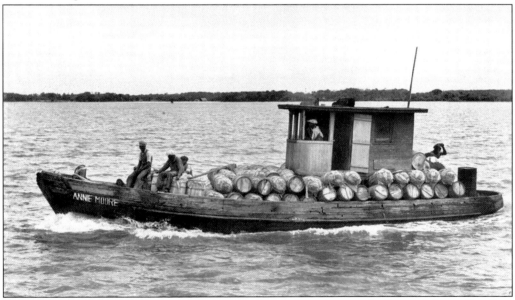

In the 1920s and 1930s, boats with names like *Annie Moore* (pictured), *Geneva Moore*, *Carolina*, *John B. Robins*, *Alligator*, *Lathrop*, and *Eva Mae* took produce from the islands to Charleston. Many of these boats were owned and operated by families like the McCabes and the Magwoods. (Courtesy of John and Teddy Walpole.)

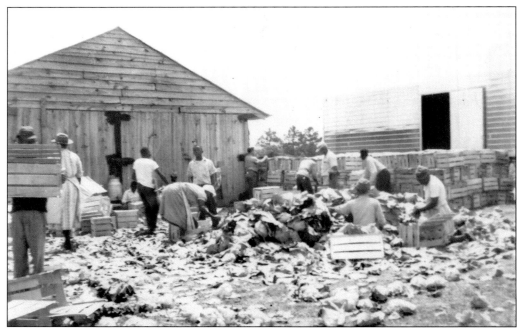

The Lowcountry was at one time known as the Cabbage Capital of the World. Boats, and later trucks, delivered cabbage to train depots, where it was shipped to northern markets. Before the days of refrigeration, railroad cars had specially designed vent systems to keep the produce cool. Later blocks of ice were placed near the vents, and air rushed over them, cooling the cabbage. The book *This Our Land, The Story of the Agricultural Society of South Carolina*, published in 1949, attributes the change from cotton production to "truck crops," or vegetables, to the insistence of Northern lenders for Southern planters to move away from cotton after the Civil War. (Bottom image courtesy of Frank Moore.)

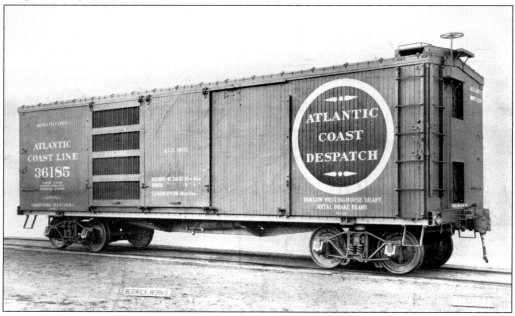

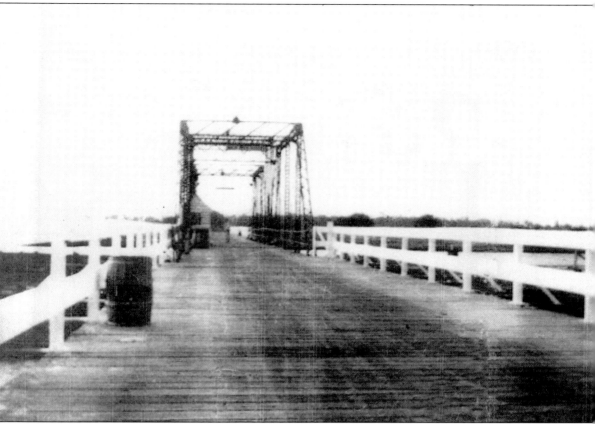

About 1930, a second bridge to the island crossed the Stono River, connecting John's Island to James Island via Maybank Highway. When it was first built, the bridge tender collected a 10¢ toll. Barrels of sand, seen at left in the photograph, were kept on the wooden creosote bridge in case of fire. The new bridge provided an alternative way for farmers to get produce to Charleston markets. Trucks gradually replaced produce boats as the primary means of transporting produce to market. (Courtesy of South Carolina Room, Charleston County Public Library.)

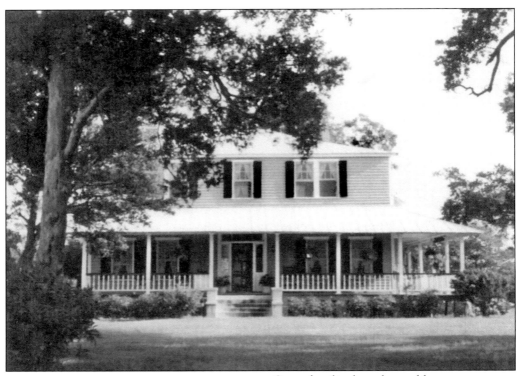

Some families have been able to preserve their old family farmhouses. This two-story country home on the Abbapoola Creek was built c. 1915 by Eugene Gordon Hay Jr. and Eliza Seabrook Hay, granddaughter of Solomon Legare. The wood clapboard house had a three-sided porch, 15-foot ceilings, and a cistern used to catch rainwater for washing clothes. The fourth and fifth generation of the family still enjoys the house today.

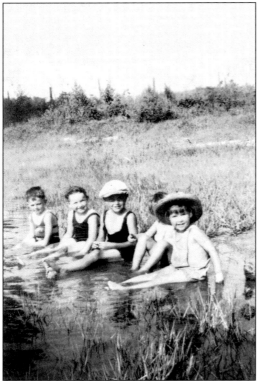

Who needs a country club? After farm chores are done, cousins (from left to right) Robert L. "Bobby" Clement, Mary, Bill, Anne, and Lydia Hay cool off in the saltwater spa near their house on the Abbapoola Creek c. 1934. (Courtesy of Charlotte and Gordon Hay.)

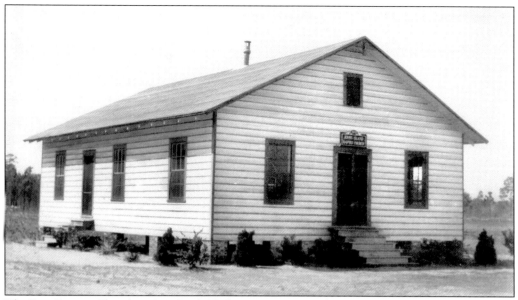

The First Baptist Church on Maybank Highway was organized in 1932. The congregation first met in Mr. Barshay's old store, on the south end of River Road, where Rev. O. M. Howe of Charleston preached the first sermon. Julius Seabrook, a merchant, gave an acre of land for a new church to be built, and in a few weeks, they raised $60 for the purchase of lumber to begin construction.

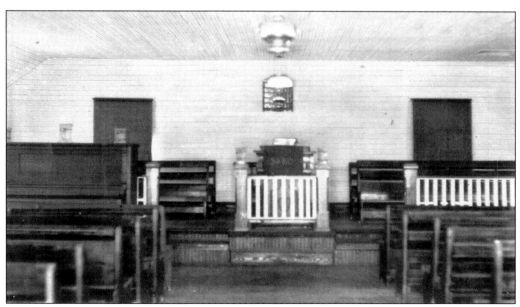

With meager incomes, most families couldn't contribute cash, so they donated services for the construction of the new church. One farmer planted an acre of corn to sell, and his wife sold eggs. One of the most generous donations was given by two black carpenters, who built the 40-foot-by-30-foot building and all the furniture for only $60. It was completed in July 1933. (Courtesy of Elizabeth Gatch Blitch.)

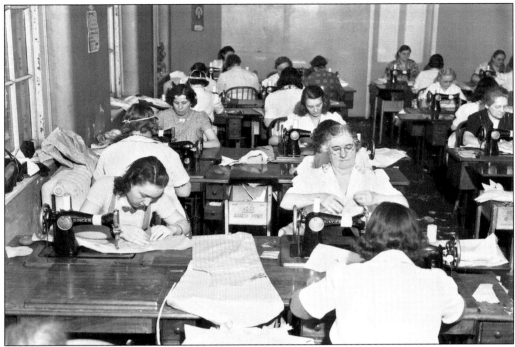

In 1935, the Works Progress Administration (WPA) was created as a relief program under the New Deal, providing jobs and income to the unemployed during the Depression. A sewing room was opened in the Agricultural Hall on Angel Oak Road, where women made clothes and were paid a weekly wage of $4.75.

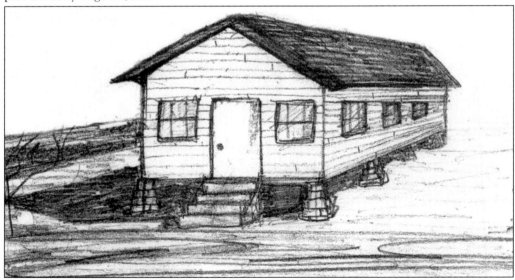

George Walter Hills deeded one acre of land to the Agricultural Society of John's Island in 1920 for the construction of the Agricultural Hall. This long wooden building was used for farmers' meetings, dances, political rallies, a temporary school, and a WPA sewing room during the Depression. When it closed in 1944, it was sold back to Hills. The building was later torn down. (Courtesy of Billy and Mary Hills.)

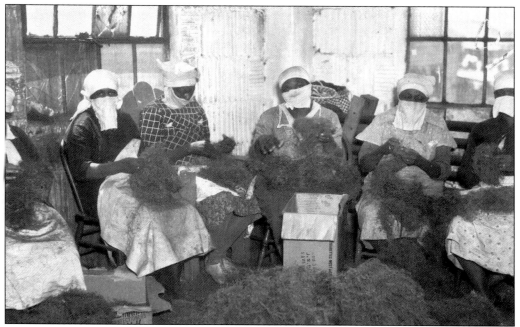

Did you know that during the 1930s there was a moss factory on the island? Factories like the one in Savannah, Georgia, pictured here were begun by the WPA in coastal areas, where Spanish moss was plentiful. Moss was gathered then "teased" by pulling it apart or rubbing it between the women's hands until all the sticks and debris were out.

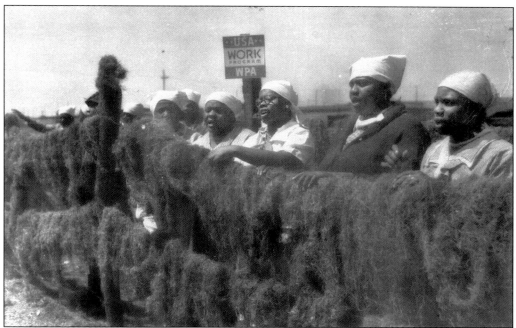

After steaming the moss for two hours to kill living organisms, the workers hung it on lines to dry in the sun. It was used to stuff mattresses, pillows, and for upholstery padding. The moss factory was on Main Road near John F. Limehouse's store.

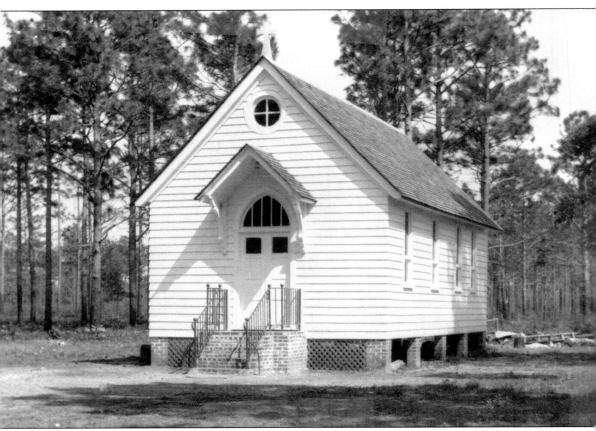

In 1939, the Roman Catholic Church of the Holy Ghost on Bohicket Road was built at a cost of $714 on land donated by E. B. Feren. There were only five catholic families on the island, so the bishop of Charleston, the Most Reverend Emmett Walsh, encouraged the cathedral to help fund construction of the church. His official coat of arms was placed inside over the door as a reminder of his support. Volunteers from all backgrounds and faiths helped the families build their church. Among the many items that were contributed are the wrought iron handrails, red-cedar shingled roof, and handmade Maltese cross on the roof. Inside the tabernacle was built of barrel staves, and the pews, communion rail, and statues were salvaged from Sacred Heart Church. Members of the founding families are buried in the graveyard behind the church along with an unknown infant who was buried there out of charity. Presently the diocese has plans to sell the property, and the fate of the beloved little church is uncertain. For over 67 years, this quaint, country church has complimented the oldest structure on the island, the Historic John's Island Presbyterian Church, built in 1719, on the opposite side of the road. (Courtesy of the Catholic Diocese of Charleston.)

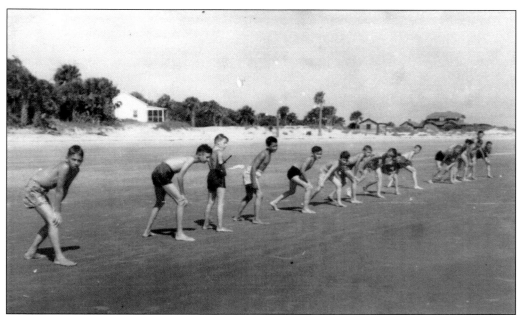

In 1934, Victor Morawetz leased part of his Seabrook Island property to the Episcopal Diocese of South Carolina, where they held their summer camp for underprivileged boys of South Carolina. Having no children of their own, Morawetz and his wife, Marjorie, decided to bequeath their land to the diocese. When Morawetz died in 1938, a codicil to his will stated his desire that the island be "a park and recreation ground and health resort for such of the public as may be in need thereof. . . . So much of the beach as can advantageously be used for healthful recreation of boys of the state of S.C. shall always be set apart for that purpose." (Courtesy of the Episcopal Diocese of South Carolina.)

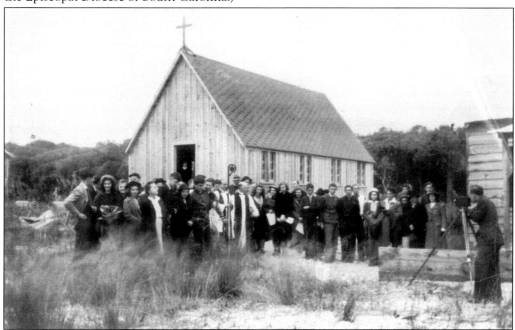

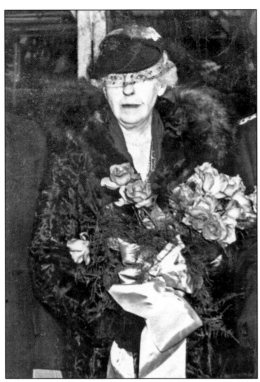

Marjorie Morawetz carried out her husband's wishes when she deeded most of Seabrook Island to the Episcopal Church, requesting the church leave unspoiled "the natural beauty of the island." (Courtesy of Stacey Draper.)

Seventeen acres, including the old "Kiawato" clubhouse shown below, were retained by Morawetz for use as her summer residence until her death in 1956. At the time, the entire island was valued at $80,000–$100,000. (Courtesy of Eleanor Jenkins.)

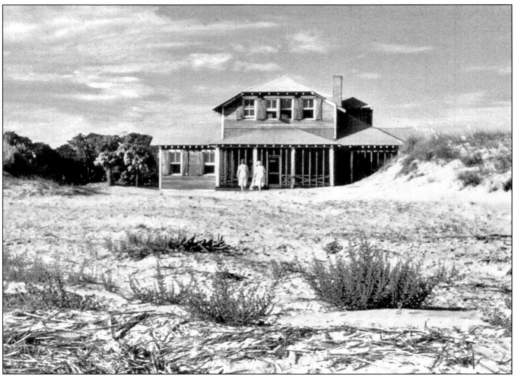

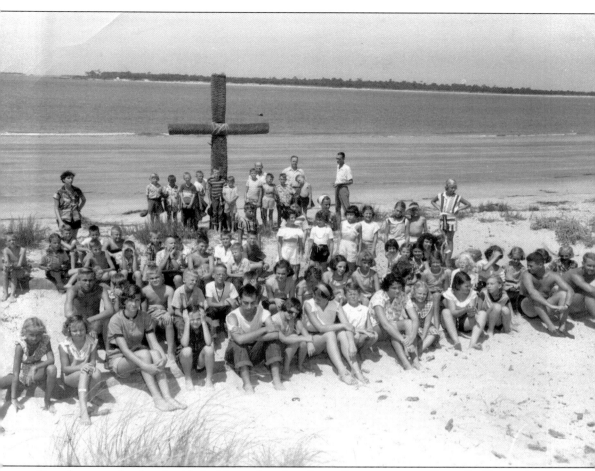

Over the years, the church added cabins, a chapel, and a conference center to Camp St. Christopher. In the late 1960s, with mounting costs of operating the camp, upgrading the facilities, and real-estate taxes on the balance of the island, the diocese decided to sell the majority of the island to Seabrook Island Company in 1971. The camp is still in operation today. The cross of palmetto logs pictured here is still a favorite spot for campers to meet. (Courtesy of the Episcopal Diocese of South Carolina.)

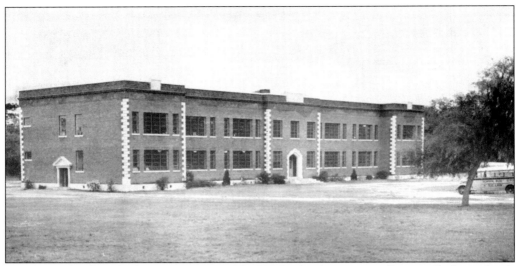

St. John's School was built in 1940 as part of the WPA schools program, allowing all white schools to be consolidated. The first classes were held in 1941 in the 13-room elementary and high school building. The old school was divided and moved, half of it used as a classroom and the other half as a cafeteria. This photograph was taken in 1944.

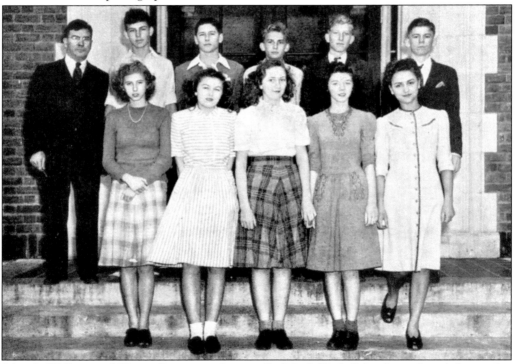

John S. Wallace and Honor Society students at St. John's High School are, from left to right, (first row) Lillian Koger, Beulah Savedge, Mildred McTeer, Ann Glover, and Mary F. Heaton; (second row) Wallace, Philip Gervais, Henry Rivers, Legare Hay, Leonard Buckner, and William Beckett. Wallace served principal then superintendent at St. John's High School. He retired in 1968 after 24 years of service to the students in school District 8.

Five
PLANTING NEW IDEAS

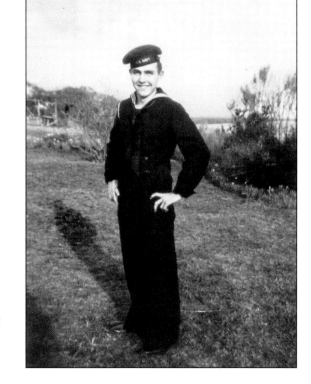

At the outbreak of World War II, many islanders left to serve in different branches of the armed forces. Pictured is William Clement Hay, who left St. John's High School in 1944 to join the navy, proudly posing in his uniform. He returned to the island and later completed his education. He worked for South Carolina Electric and Gas for 38 years and retired in 1989. (Courtesy of Lydia Hay Pedersen.)

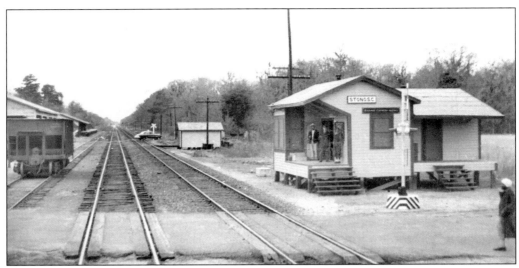

The Stono Depot was built after the Seaboard Air Line Railroad (SAL) expanded its service from Charleston to Savannah in 1916. SAL built all but two of the produce sheds that sat near its tracks off Main Road across from where the Stono Market Café is today. The SAL trains ran from Hamlet, North Carolina, to Savannah, Georgia. Produce sheds (pictured at left) owned by local farmers were built close to the tracks so they could ship produce to other markets. (Courtesy of Frank Moore.)

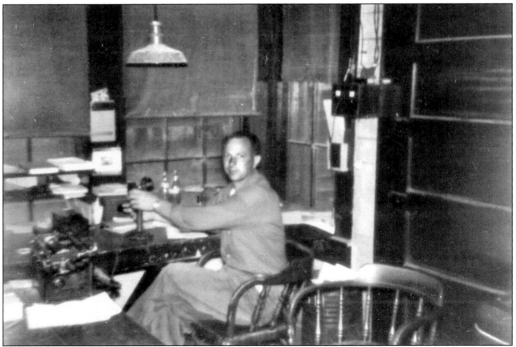

Frank Howard Sr., seen here in 1950, was the Stono Depot agent from 1941 to the early 1970s for SAL. He handled all depot operations, including receiving daily train orders and schedules. During World War II, Howard received the order to allow trains transporting troops to pass without delay. (Courtesy of Frank L. Howard Jr.)

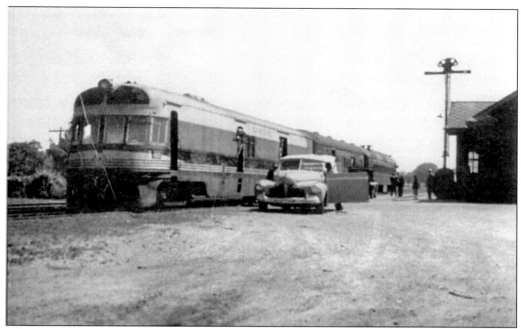

The Seaboard train (Nos. 25 and 26) was nicknamed the "Boll Weevil" and was a popular passenger train. It departed Hamlet, North Carolina, at 8:30 a.m. and stopped at every station along the way, including any trackside location where it was flagged down. Passengers could ride for 10¢. Passenger service was discontinued by 1956. (Courtesy of Frank Moore.)

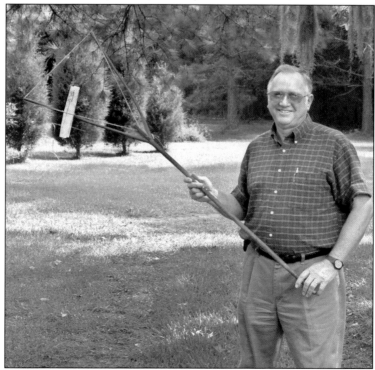

The Stono Depot agent, Frank Howard Sr. lived right across the road from the depot. His son, Frank Leaman Howard Jr., and his brothers still live on John's Island and remember how the station operations ran. Howard demonstrates how his father passed train orders from the depot platform to the conductor of the moving train. (Photographer Billy Rutherford.)

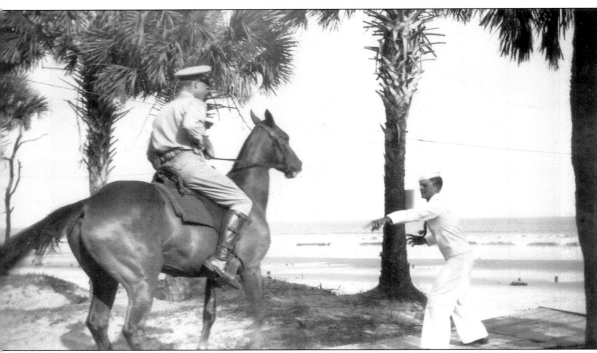

During World War II, the U.S. Coast Guard operated beach patrols on Kiawah and Seabrook. Guards occupied the Vanderhorst house on Kiawah Island and Camp St. Christopher on Seabrook Island, and visitors were restricted from the beaches. Guards patrolled the beaches on horseback and in Jeeps. Lester (Ed) Stringer of James Island served in the Coast Guard c. 1943, and his daughter, Gretchen Stringer of James Island, contributed this photograph from his album.

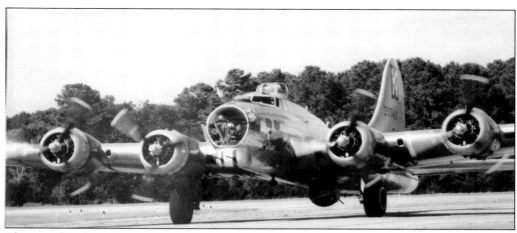

This B-17 bomber, photographed by Bob Gilbert in recent times, is like the ones that practiced at the John's Island Military Airfield during World War II. In August 1943, the U.S. government leased approximately 900 acres of the former Saxby and Bosomworth plantations from Charleston County and bought 400 more from adjacent property owners to build an airfield on the island. In 1944–1945, the John's Island Airfield Military Reservation was constructed in only 95 days. It served as an auxiliary training base but was also used as a take-off point for transatlantic flights. In 1948, Charleston County took over the operation and maintenance of the airport until 1975, when it was transferred to the Charleston County Aviation Authority and became Charleston Executive Airport. (Copyright: Bob Gilbert.)

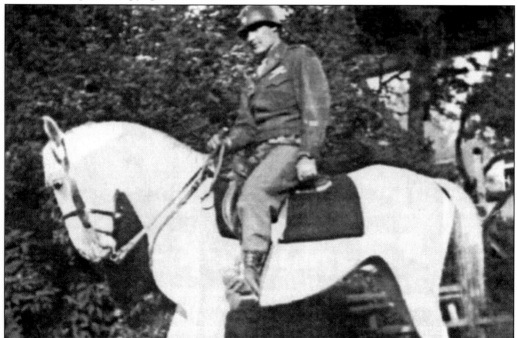

During World War II, Lt. Col. Charles B. Bryan Sr., whose farm was on Bryan Dairy Road, served as a member of the infantry from 1940 to 1945. "Mr. Charlie," as he was affectionately known around the island, was highly decorated for his valiant service in the European theater. His wife, Amelia, and some of their children still live on the farm. (Courtesy of Amelia Bryan.)

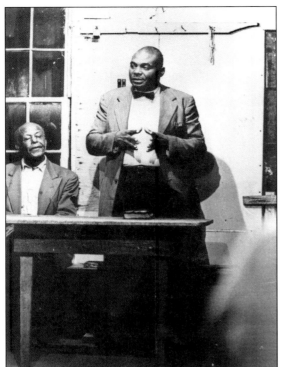

After World War II, the civil rights movement gained momentum. Island native Esau Jenkins (1910–1972) was one of the movement's notable leaders, recognizing the value of education for the black community. He quit school in the fourth grade to help his family work, and later attended night school taught by visiting clergyman Rev. Giles Brown. He had a successful vegetable business in Charleston and, with the aid of Bernice Robinson and Septima Clark, helped start the first citizenship schools. (Courtesy of photographer Robert Yellin.)

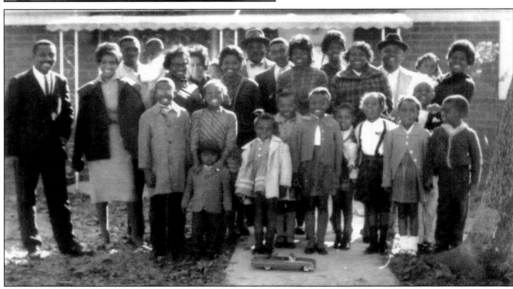

Three generations of Esau Jenkins' family are pictured here in 1961. From left to right are (first row) Gilbert Grimball Jr. and Gilberta Grimball; (second row) Leonard Jenkins, Elaine Jenkins, Jackie Grimball, Cathy Jenkins, Marnishia, Beverly Jenkins, Abe Jenkins, Andrea Jones, and Ezekiel Jones Jr.; (third row) Georgetta Jenkins, Ethel Grimball, Emma Jenkins, Francena Buncomb, Janie Jenkins, Maxine Jones (baby), and M. Jones; (fourth row) James Jenkins, Abraham Jenkins Sr., Kenneth Jenkins (baby), Alfreda Jenkins, Esau Jenkins, Gilbert Grimball Sr., Loretta Saunders, and Ezekiel Jones Sr. (Courtesy of Bill Jenkins.)

After World War II, a new class of sailboats, the Sea Island One Designs, were built to standardize the racing among the various island yacht clubs. The Sea Island One Designs were the result of Oliver Seabrook sending three sketches to a naval architect in the Northeast who drew the final design. The first boats were named *Cygnet* (James Island), *Undine* (Wadmalaw), *Doghouse*, and *Marcheta* (John's Island). They are still racing today. Racing *Marcheta* in this 1948 photograph are James Simons, Philip Walpole, and Eugene Walpole Jr.

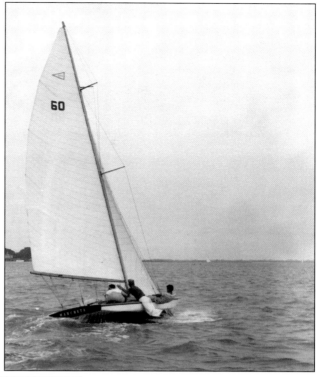

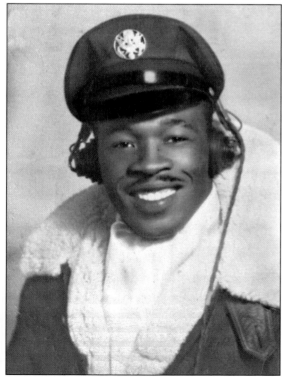

William "Bill" Jenkins, a John's Island native, graduated from Alabama State University in 1951. He joined the airforce, enlisted for 2 years and then served as an officer for 18 years. He is presently a lay leader for the United Methodist Church of the Charleston, South Carolina, District and on the board of directors for Rural Missions on John's Island, where he served as administrator (Courtesy of Anna Fields White.)

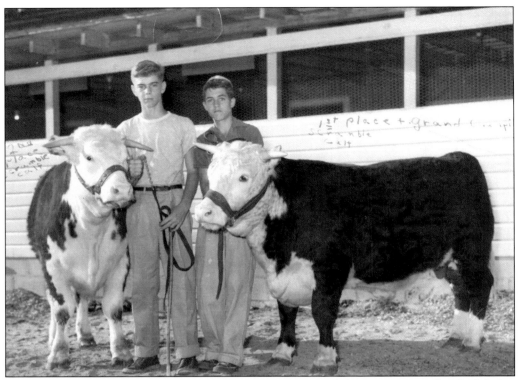

Four-H clubs were organized at St. John's School, and young farmers participated in competitions at the county fair. Edward Hay (above, left) of Wadmalaw and Legare Walpole of John's Island placed second and first, respectively, with their "scramble" calves. Each year, young calves were released as boys and girls scrambled to catch one. They raised the calf until the following year, when it was auctioned off at the fair. Some calves brought as much as $700. Ed Hay became an orthopedic hand surgeon in Charleston, and Legare Walpole operated a family farm and Abbapoola Sod Farm, which his son runs today. (Courtesy of Charleston *Post and Courier*.)

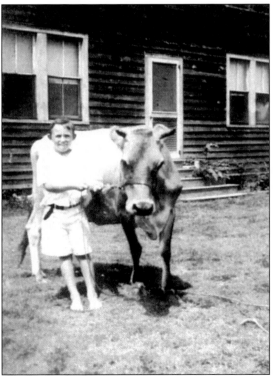

Some farm boys left the island but took their farm roots with them. Gordon Hay is pictured as a young boy with one of his cows. He retired in 1995 as executive vice president and corporate secretary of Coburg Dairy, Inc. (Courtesy of Charlotte and Gordon Hay.)

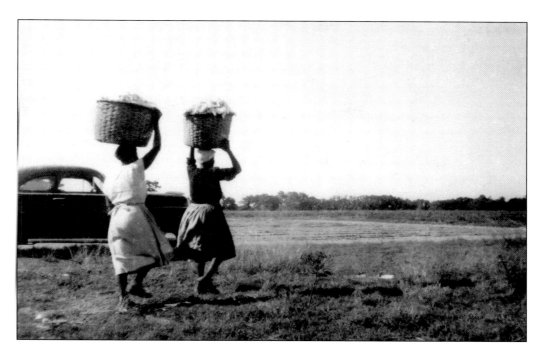

Truck farming began to expand in the 1950s and 1960s as modern equipment and new methods increased crop yield. New varieties of short-staple cotton and other crops were tried by island farmers. In the photograph above, Evelina Smith (front) and Ella Reed carry baskets of cotton from the field at Sunnyside Farms on River Road around 1950. Benji Pickney is pictured below in the cotton truck.

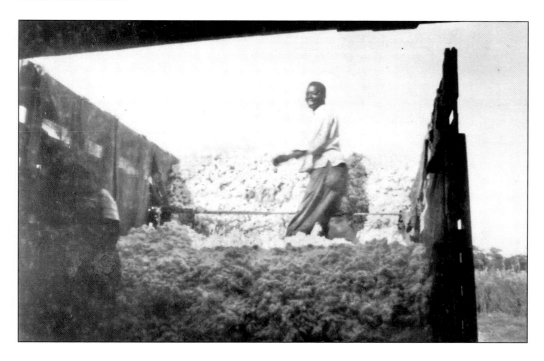

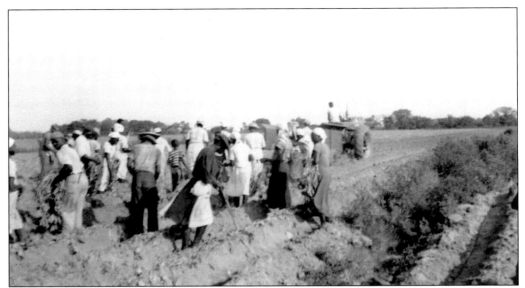

Sweet potatoes were another popular truck crop. They still required a great deal of manual labor. Potato "slips" or roots were dropped on top of the prepared bed as another worker followed behind, pushing the slip into the ground and covering it with soil.

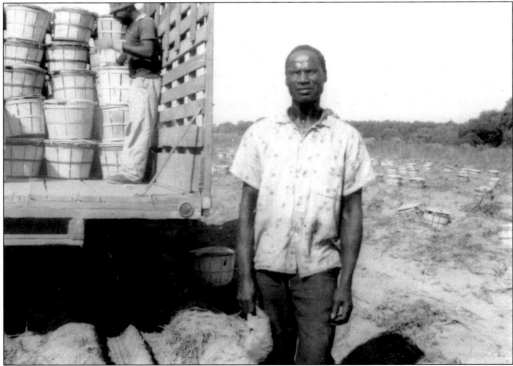

At harvest, sweet potatoes were gathered into bushel baskets and stored in curing houses until they sweetened and were ready for market. Other farmers "banked" their potatoes, using layers of cornhusks and hay topped with soil. Enoch Johnson and Thomas McNeil (on truck) are shown loading baskets of sweet potatoes.

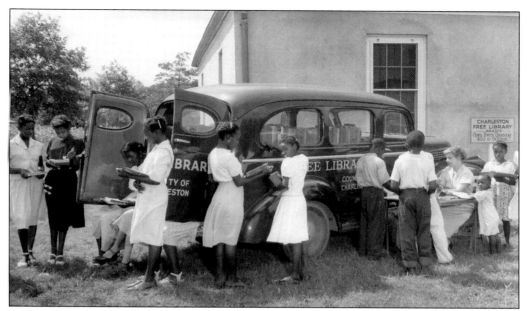

In 1931, the Charleston County Library began a mobile library service to reach families in rural areas. The John's Island Rural Community Center, seen here in 1950, was a regular stop. It is now the Headstart Development Center on Bohicket Road. (Courtesy of South Carolina Room, Charleston County Public Library.)

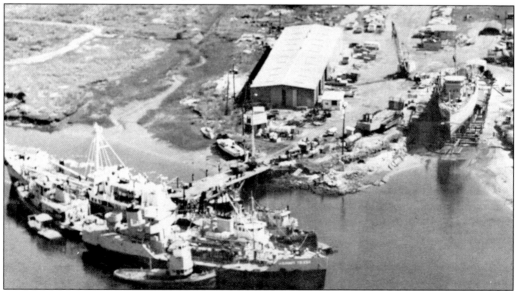

Arthur Ross Swygert Sr. brought a new business, named Sandblasters, to the banks of the Stono in 1956, when he began a ship repair and sandblasting operation primarily serving the military. When the shipyard in North Charleston closed in 1992, he added a yacht repair service. After his death in 2004, his children and grandchildren continued running the business, which was renamed Ross Marine. The business celebrated its 50th anniversary in 2006. It is located off River Road. A huge propeller marks the turn on Swygert Boulevard. This photograph dates from the 1950s.

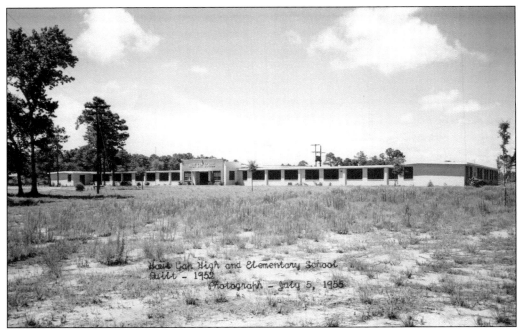

Esau Jenkins was influential in having black schools consolidated in the 1950s, and a new high school, Haut Gap, located on Bohicket Road, was completed in 1952. It is presently Haut Gap Middle School.

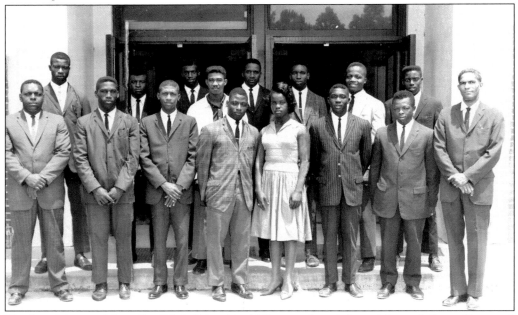

The bus drivers at Haut Gap High School in 1962 were, from left to right, as follows: (first row) coach Nathaniel Cook, Thomas Frazier, Josie Bishop, Robert Fields Jr., Edna Grimball, James Edward Lee, Mason Heyward, and principal John Scott; (second row) Jimmy Wigfall, unidentified, unidentified, Roy LaRoche, unidentified, unidentified, Carl Brown, and unidentified. (Courtesy of Anna Fields White.)

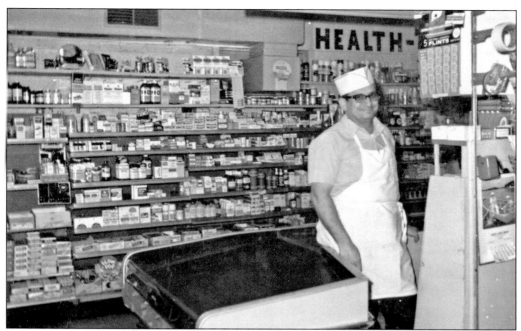

Farming was prospering in 1947, when James Eddie Koger opened Koger's General Merchandise Store on River Road three quarters of a mile south of Maybank Highway. He added a hardware store and sold everything from crab lines to chain saws. Ernest (above) and Annie Laurie Koger, who bought the grocery store in 1957, knew all their customers by name.

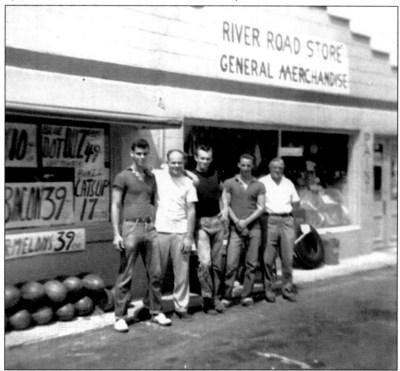

A number of young people from the island were employed at Koger's store. Seen here are, from left to right, James Seabrook, Jerold Anderson, and Larry, Johnny, and Ronald Benton. The Kogers sold their businesses when they retired in the 1970s, but they will always be remembered for their personal customer service. (Photographs courtesy of Ernest and Annie Laurie Koger.)

THE BRIDLE PATH TO

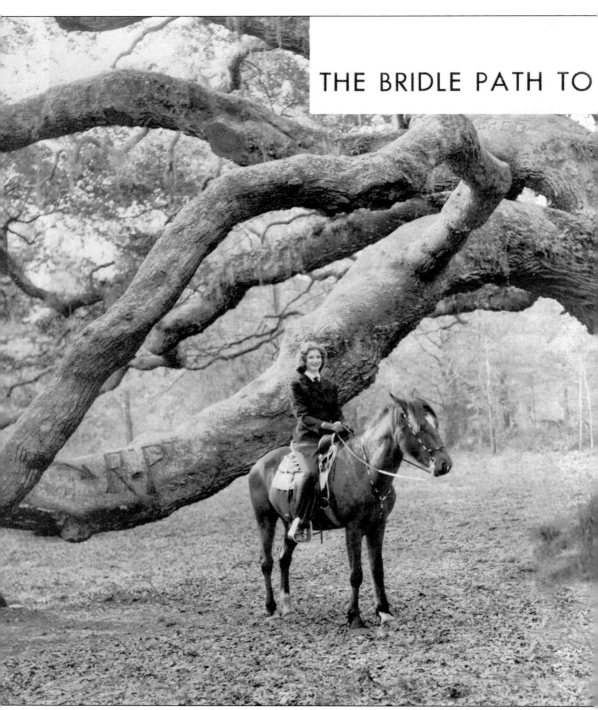

The Angel Oak is a live oak (*Quercus virginiana*) and is believed to be one of the oldest and largest trees in the country. It is 65 feet tall, has a circumference of 25.5 feet, a shade area of 17,000 square feet, a length of 89 feet, and its largest limb has a circumference of 11.5 feet. It is a nationally recognized landmark and named for the Angel family, whose plantation once

Our Features

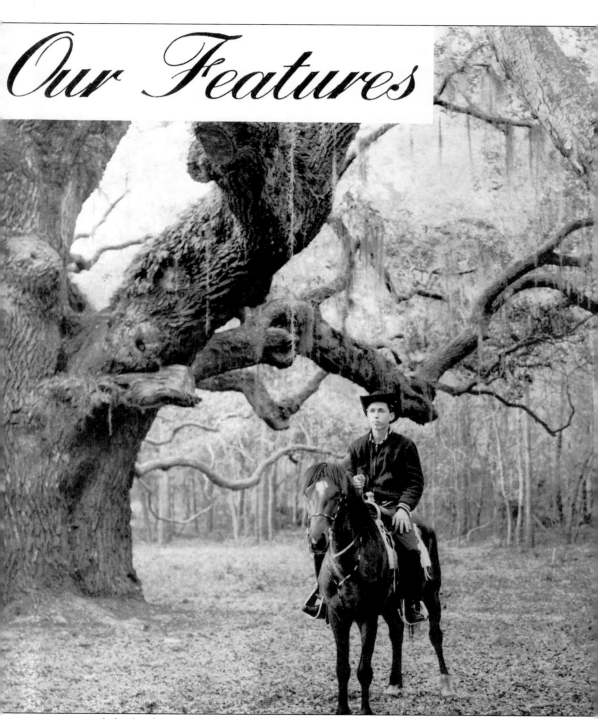

encompassed the land upon which it is located. It is open to the public free of charge. In the late 1980s, it was the center of controversy in an eminent domain battle between the City of Charleston and its private owner. This photograph from the St. John's High School yearbook in 1960 shows Marianne Seabrook and Wendell Weeks at the Angel Oak.

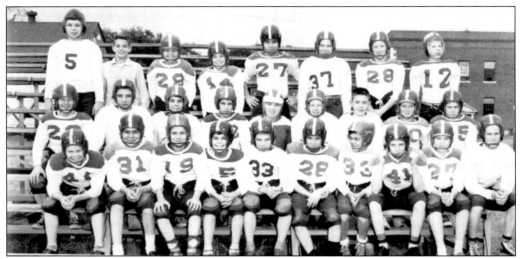

A new crop of St. John's Islanders in 1956 included Charles Ayer, Martin Meyer, Steve Metts, Billy Ayer, Ray Spieghts, David Boyer, Frank Meyer, Jimmie Dickinson, Otis Lee Sanders, Charles Mains, Homer Davis, Fancis Heffron, Gerald Anderson, Ernest Koger, Mac Martin, Ted King, Jack Limehouse, Bruce Humbert, Louis Andrews, Frank Burkhart, Billy Suggs, Kenneth Thomas, Caroll Suggs, Roy Metts, Charles Smoak, Buddy Bryan, and Lewis Hay.

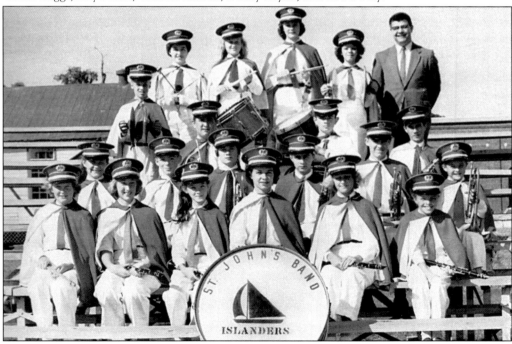

The 1959 St. John's High School marching band was directed by Mac McCauley. Pictured from left to right are (first row) Carolyn Brant, Meemee Bryan, Jane Hills, Mary Britton, Margaret Brant, and Lyn Harrison; (second row) Judy Collins, Jimmy Momier, Sally Hart, Andy Britton, Joe Momier, and Bobby Bentz; (third row) Billy Hilton, Luther Corley, Mike Hunt, and Philip Bryan; (fourth row) Katherine Fowler, Margaret Seabrook, Charlene Collins, Ann Hempton, and Mac McCauley, director. (Courtesy of St. John's High School.)

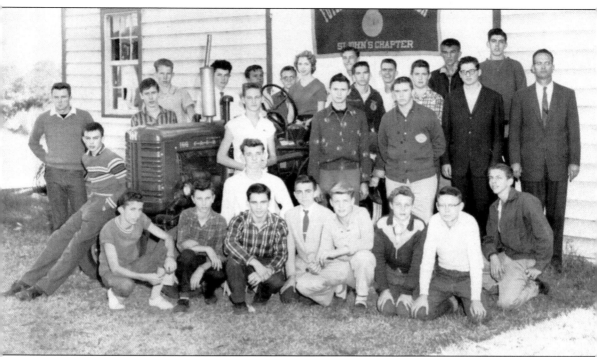

Future Farmers of America at St. John's High School in 1959 included Chris Davis, R. Speights, Larry Glover, Pete Cumbee, Kenneth Thomas, Andy Britton, Trap Seabrook, Roy Spain, Billy Strogier, Albert Thompson, Rodney Barnwell, Tommy King, Donald Richter, Buddy Davis, Beth Hills, Charlie Smoak, Billy Sylvester, Billy Hilton, Martin Myer, Elliott Harris, Harold Bennett, and teacher Lucius Platt. (Courtesy of St. John's High School.)

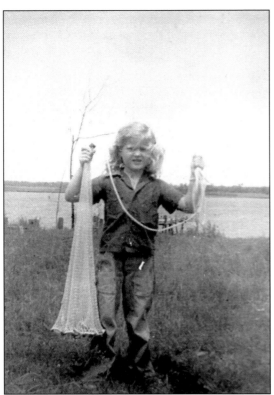

Nothing goes better with grits than shrimp. Margaret Seabrook, age six, poses with the small cast net her father, Mash Seabrook, made for her in 1954. Her grandfather John Seabrook grew sugarcane and other crops on his farm on the Stono River, seen behind her. (Courtesy of Margaret Seabrook.)

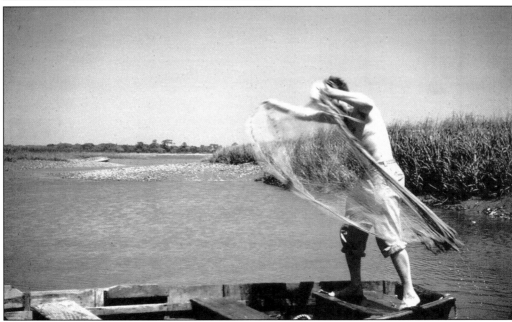

Summertime activities on the island center around the water. D. F. Jenkins casts for shrimp in 1960 in Abbapoola Creek. Some men on the island made cast nets, which was an intricate skill. Throwing a cast net properly is also a skill to be acquired. (Courtesy of Eleanor Jenkins.)

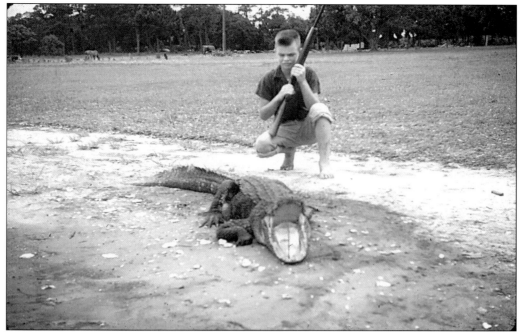

A young Skipper Bentz is pictured with an alligator that wandered away from its riverbank on his grandparents' farm. Skipper Bentz grew up to own Botany Bay Boat Repair Service. The alligator became a pair of shoes, a wallet, and a belt. (Courtesy of June Walpole Dickerson.)

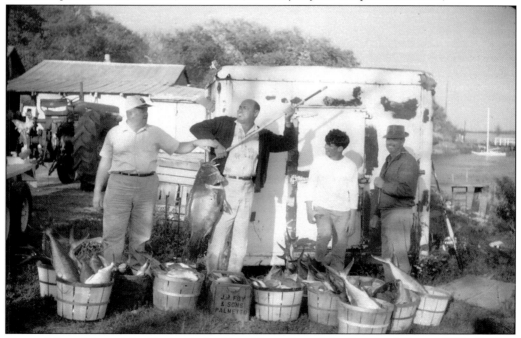

Pictured from left to right, Benjamin Jenkins, Henry Rast, John Rast, and George Hills divide a big catch. In those days, there were no limits on catches and no limits on the stories told afterward. Reportedly, with these men, the big one never got away. (Courtesy of Eleanor Jenkins.)

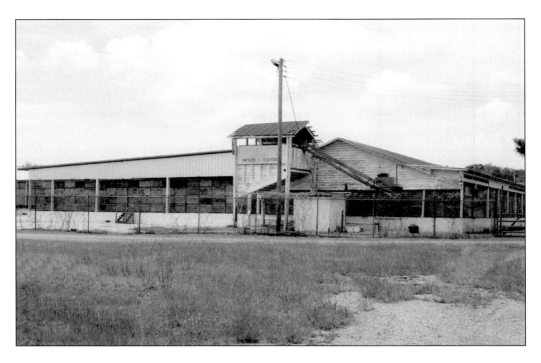

Tomatoes became the hot new crop on the island. Seen here is the old Stonoco packing and shipping shed on Main Road next to the train depot. Tomatoes were picked and put in heavy wooden crates like those seen here on the truck on the Jenkinses' farm. (Courtesy of Eleanor Jenkins.)

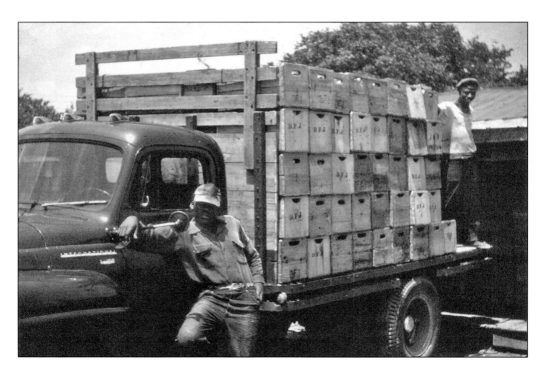

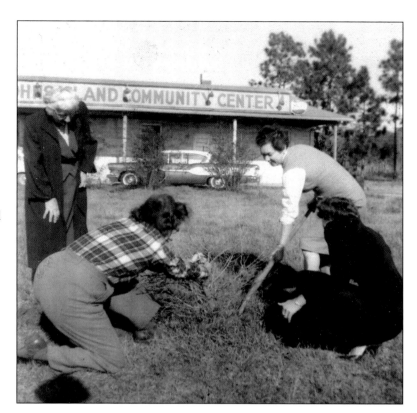

The ladies of the Magnolia Garden Club have worked to preserve the beauty of John's Island for future generations since 1952. In the past, their projects have included landscaping schools, tending the grounds around the Angel Oak, and helping preserve Deveaux Bank at the mouth of North Edisto River just off Seabrook Island. Members are seen in this 1958 photograph planting dogwood trees at the John's Island Community Center on Maybank Highway.

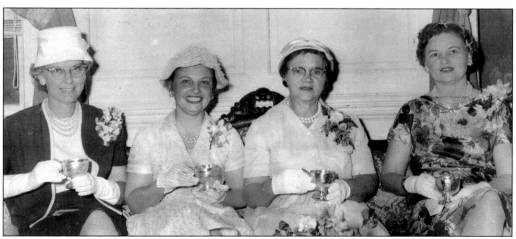

The hardworking ladies of the Magnolia Garden Club celebrate at the 10th anniversary tea in 1962 at the home of Mrs. K. B. Kerr. Club officers pictured left to right are Mrs. R. A. Madsen, Mrs. W. S. Allan, Mrs. T. A Price, and Mrs. H. L. Glover. The club is still active today. (Courtesy of Guerry Glover.)

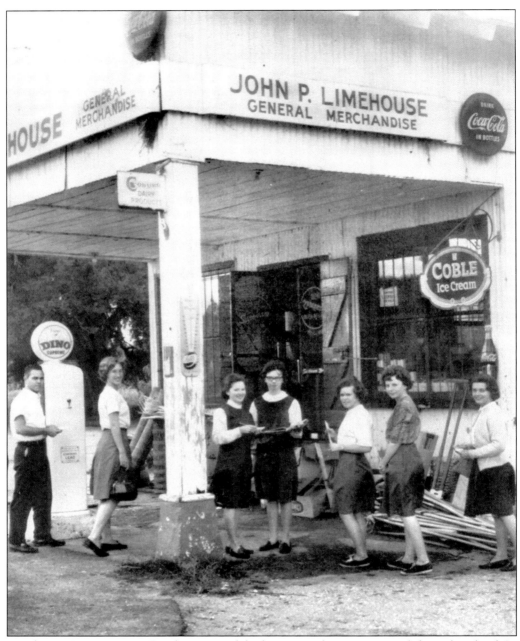

Limehouse Store on Main Road was one of the last original country stores left on the island. In this 1964 photograph, students of St. John's High School enjoy the nostalgia of the old store. Only the Butcher Oak, which was next to the store, remains today. From left to right are Jeffy Stutts, Meemee Bryan, Geraldine Davis, Anne Hempton, Betty Lou Crouch, Renee Coleman, and Anne Lackey. (Courtesy of St. John's High School.)

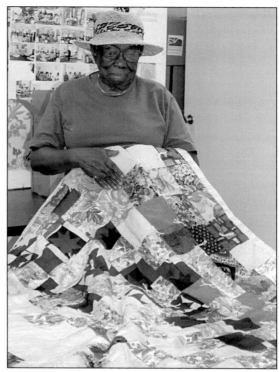

Many retirees with lower incomes now have more options available to them to live their last years in familiar surroundings close to old friends. The Sea Island Comprehensive Health Care Corporation runs a rural housing program, providing homes for handicapped individuals and seniors citizens. Marie McPherson Grant, born in 1914, has lived and worked on John's Island all her life. She and her husband had 12 children, five of whom died. She made this beautiful quilt to donate to the senior center. (Photographer Billy Rutherford.)

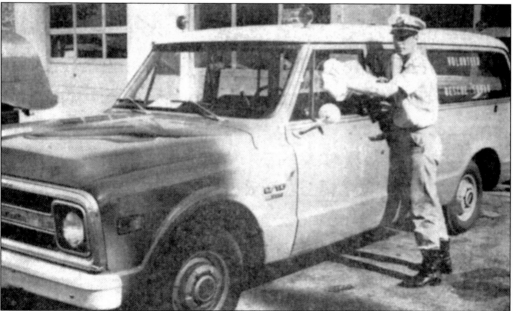

The St. John's Fire District was established in 1959. Assistant Fire Chief John W. Weeks Jr. is seen here with a new ambulance that the community helped the fire department buy in 1969 to serve John's and Wadmalaw Islands. The John's Island Fire Department continues to serve the rapidly growing community with professionalism and proficiency. They presently have six stations that serve Kiawah, Seabrook, Wadmalaw, and John's Island. (Courtesy of Gary Glover.)

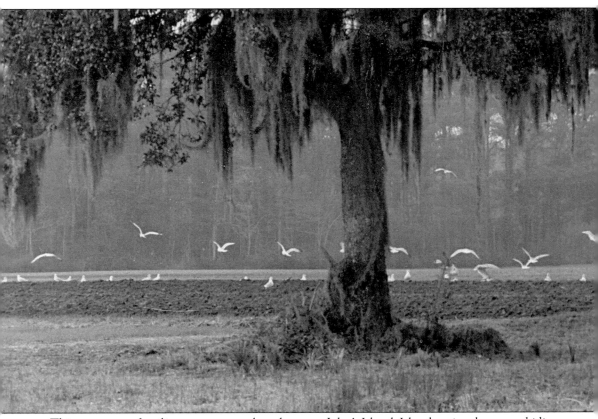
This was once a familiar scene on rural roadways on John's Island. Island natives have an abiding appreciation for the smell of a freshly plowed field and the beauty of a morning mist rising over

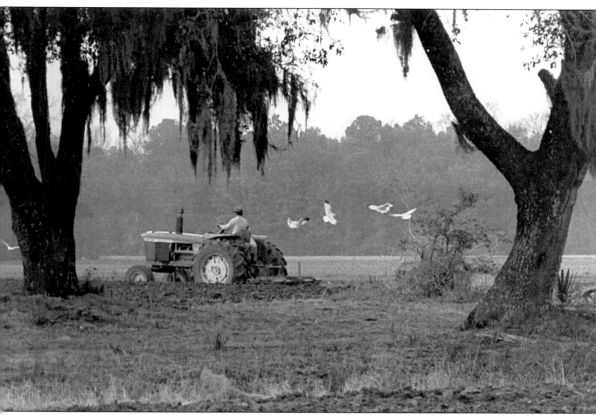
it. In this photograph, Bruce Tyler is plowing a field on Wingate Farm off River Road. (Courtesy of Charleston *Post and Courier*.)

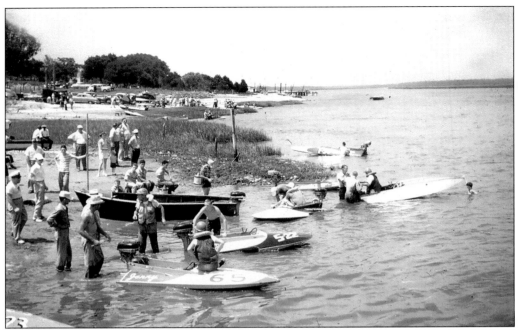

Something faster than sailboats was seen racing at Rockville in the 1950s and 1960s. John's Island boys competed against boats from neighboring Wadmalaw and James Islands. Some were up to nine feet in length and capable of speeds of up to 60 to 80 miles per hour. Though considered risky by some, fortunately there was never a serious injury. (Courtesy of Eleanor Jenkins.)

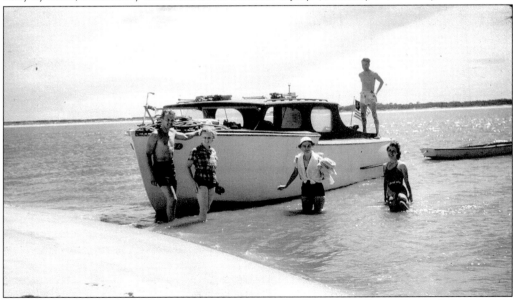

Friends enjoy a day at Bird Key, located at the mouth of the Stono River. Sandy Point, seen in the background on the north end of Kiawah, is another favorite destination for a day's boating trip. Bird Key is an important nesting area for brown pelicans and now has access limitations. From left to right are Earl Van Fleet, Irene Fletcher, Eleanor Jenkins, Jane Van Fleet, and Teddy Fletcher standing on the boat.

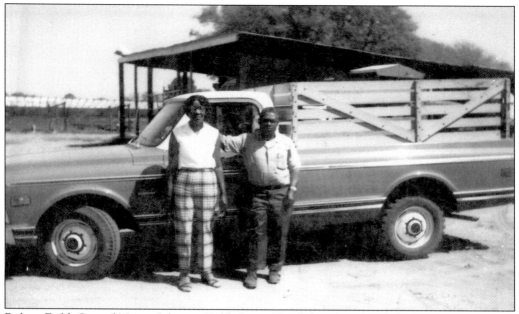

Robert Fields Sr. and Nancy Johnson Fields farmed land that their family had since 1911. Nancy Fields opened a community store in 1957 on River Road, which her daughter, Anna Fields White, still runs the store today. They raised eight children, some of who still farm the land. (Courtesy of Anna Fields White.)

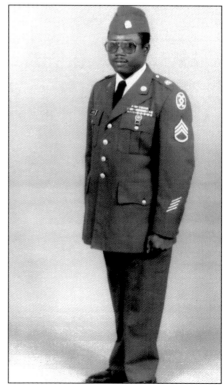

Besides eight of their own, the Johnsons raised grandson Philip Johnson, seen at the right during the time he served in Vietnam as a noncommissioned officer. He graduated from St. John's High School in 1969, and after Vietnam, he served in the U.S. Army Reserves for almost 30 years. He returned to John's Island and now serves as supervisor of the sanitation department on James Island. (Courtesy of Ella Johnson Walker.)

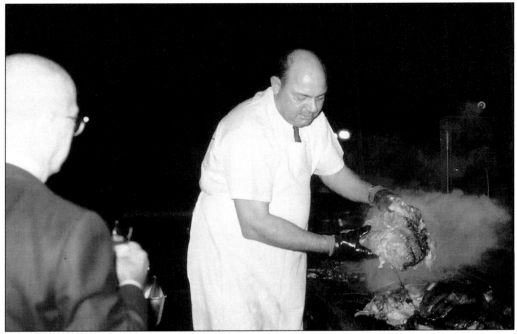

Farmer Henry Rast, famous for his delicious barbecue, was often asked to cook for countless benefits around the island. He started out using box springs to cook enough meat for big crowds and got up at 3 a.m. to begin cooking. (Courtesy of Ada Seabrook Rast.)

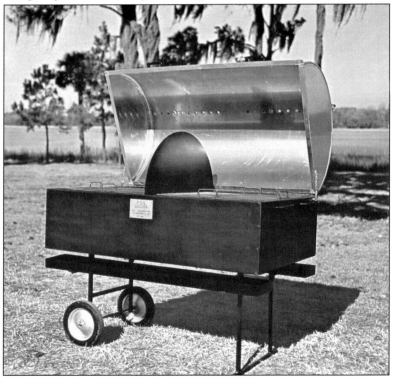

After much trial and error, Rast invented a fast barbecue cooker and had it patented in 1968 under the name *PDQ Cooker*, for "pretty damn quick." Even high-end stores like Neiman Marcus in New York and Atlanta sold PDQ Cookers. His son, Tuffy, opened the first full-service restaurant on John's Island, located on Bohicket Road near the Presbyterian church. He now owns Tuffy's Produce on Highway 17.

Six

HARVEST OF CHANGE

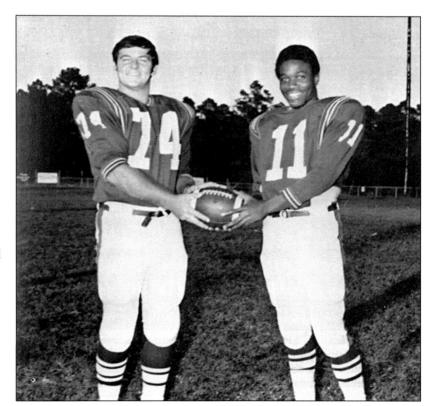

The 1970s brought new opportunities and integration to the public schools. St. John's High School's first racially integrated football team went 8-2 in the 1970 season, displaying islanders' ability to handle change. Pictured are senior linebacker Mike Hutson (left) and senior tailback Robert Bonneau. The head coach that year was the legendary Bob Biggerstaff.

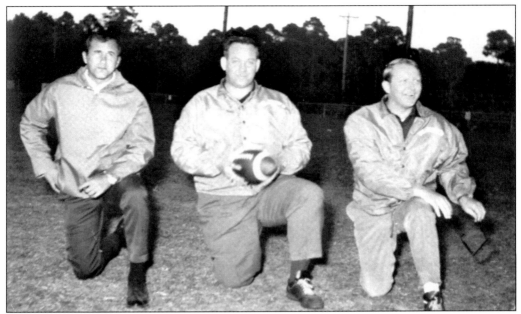

Head football coach Bob Biggerstaff (center) retired in 1998 after coaching for 33 years at St. John's High School. Assistant coaches pictured are Randy Castle (left) and Richard Goehring (right). In his third year, 1968, they won the state championship and Biggerstaff was named South Carolina Coach of the Year. His teams were conference champs 18 times.

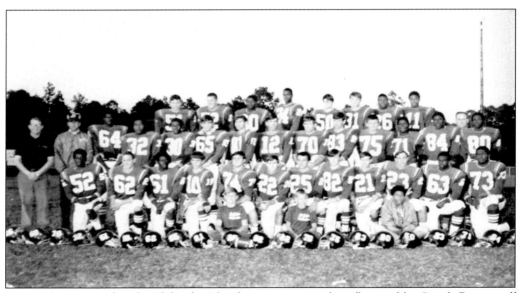

Many young men who played for the Islanders were positively influenced by Coach Biggerstaff and his excellent assistants. A good many of his players went on to play college ball at major colleges, and some even made it to the National Football League (see page 111). Because of his influence on and off the field, the football field at St. John's is named in his honor. (Courtesy of Bob Biggerstaff.)

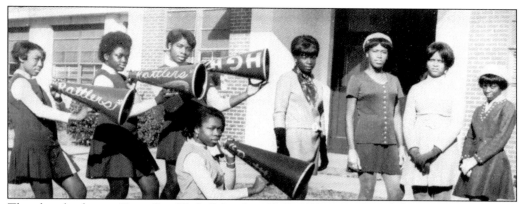

The cheerleaders at Haut Gap High School in 1969–1970 were, from left to right, (standing) Albertha Frasier, Geraldine Wilson, Janet Frasier, Easter Hymes, Beulah Brown, Rose Marie Lawyer, and Angela Nelson. Kneeling is Bernice Greene.

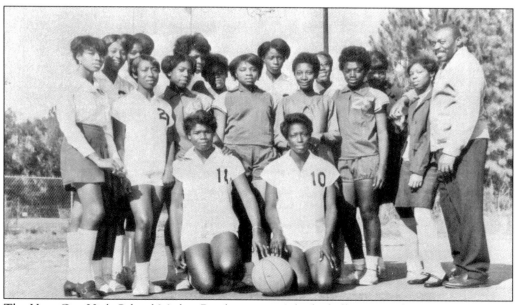

The Haut Gap High School Mighty Rattlers women's basketball team in the 1969–1970 school year was coached by Rev. Eddie L. Jackson. Included here are Christine Green, Dianne Chisolm, Mary Washington, Bertha Frasier, Albertha Cohen, Hattie Washington, Evelina Freeman, Virginia Brown, Arlene Joyner, Ruby Deas, Daisey Brisbane, Geraldine Wilson, Delores Simmons, and Janice Jones.

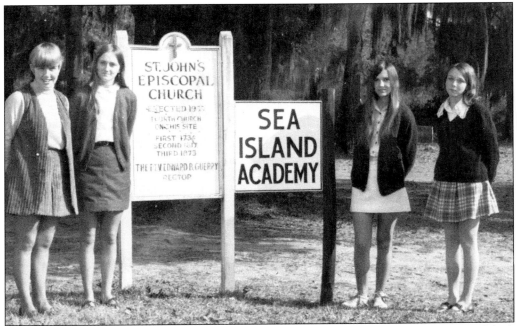

In 1970, Sea Island Academy was organized and held classes for grades 7 through 12 at St. John's Episcopal Church on Maybank Highway. In 1971, the small private school elected to merge with Sea Island Baptist School, which had held classes for elementary grades since 1966 at First Baptist Church of John's Island. Pictured from left to right are Jaye Oliver, Debbie Corbett, Vickie Leland, and Lynn Thompson.

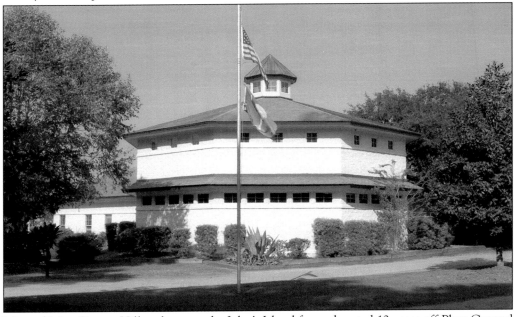

Mr. and Mrs. George Hills, who owned a John's Island farm, donated 12 acres off Plow Ground Road for Sea Island Academy to build a new school in 1972. The name was changed to Charleston Collegiate in 2001. (Photographer Billy Rutherford.)

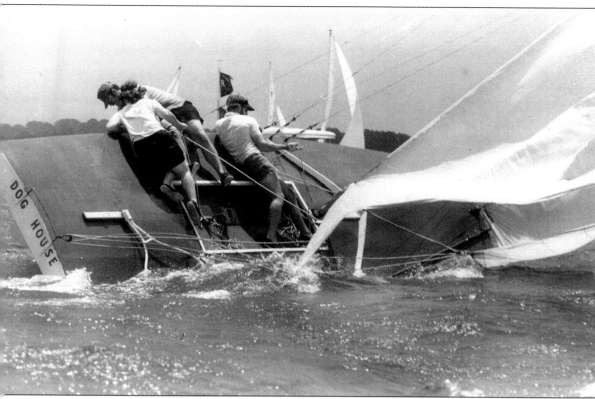

A second generation of sailors continued sailing Sea Island One Designs. Margaret Seabrook Wofford, Danny Wofford, and Neil Edgerton prepare for an apparent capsize on the Sea Island One Design *Doghouse* in 1979. The *Doghouse* got its name from Sam Seabrook, who was afraid he was going to be in the doghouse when his wife Mary Ellen found out he was having it built by Carl Glover (who also built *Marcheta*). He was right, and the name stuck. The *Doghouse* recovered in the incident pictured above and went on to win the race. The Sea Island One Design class has been revived with the addition of four new boats in recent decades. At the end of the local regatta season, the boat with the best cumulative performance wins the Ellis Trophy at the conclusion of the Rockville Regatta. (Courtesy of photographers Mike and Anne Adair.)

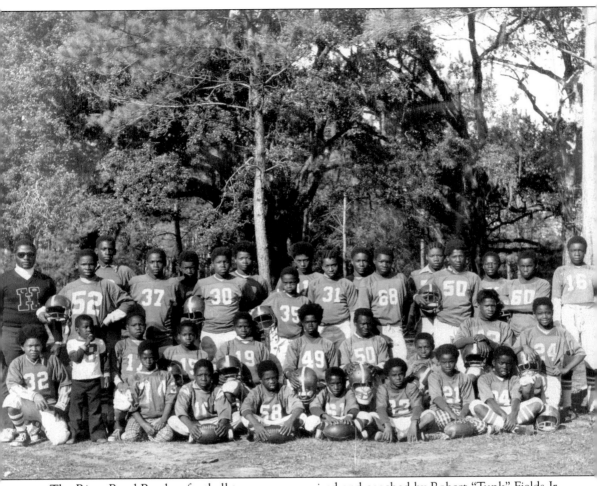

The River Road Rattlers football team was organized and coached by Robert "Tunk" Fields Jr. Pictured are, from left to right, (first row) Herman Wine Jr., Thomas McNeil, Antoine Saunders, Mark Middleton, David Givens, Darrel Givens, and Aaron Givens; (second row) Wayne Stroude, Cedrick Fields, Jacob Brown Jr., Kevin Fields, Joseph Smiley, Lennard Pinckney, Anthony Grant, John Brown, Jeff Stanley, and Irvin Goodwin; (third row) Robert Fields, David Hunter, Darnell Wine, Timmy Goodwin, Christopher Brown, Gary Jenkins, George Simmons, Laurence Middleton, James Jenkins, and Jesse Brown; (fourth row) Larry Wine, James Brown, Henry Pinckney, Clifford Hammond, Buster Wright, David Brown, and Gregory Grant. (Courtesy of Robert Fields.)

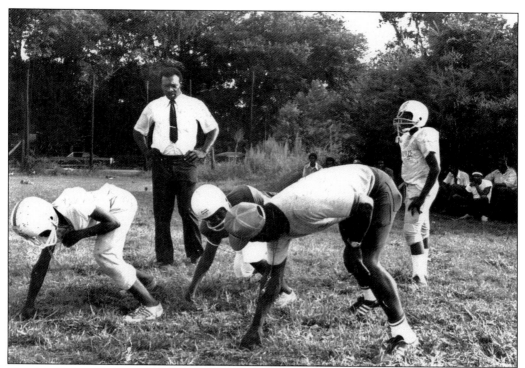

Coaches Robert Fields and Bill Jenkins practice with their River Road Rattlers. Future NFL player Charlie Brown is the center of this early 1970s photograph.

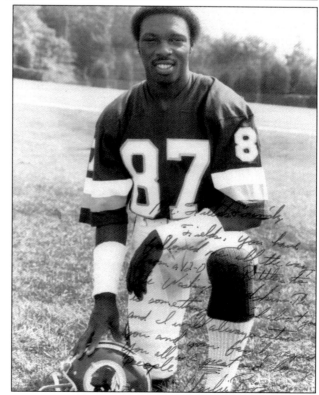

John's Island native Charlie Brown, seen at right, played for Coach Biggerstaff at St. John's High School, in college at South Carolina State University, and in the NFL for the Washington Redskins, where he was a key player in the 1983 and 1984 Super Bowls. He later played for Atlanta and Indianapolis. He is presently coaching and teaching in Savannah, Georgia. (Courtesy of Robert Fields.)

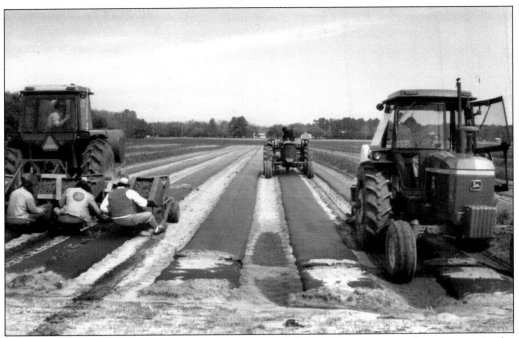

In the 1970s and 1980s, John's Island became one of the largest tomato-producing areas in the state. New planting methods using black plastic retained soil moisture, controlled weeds, and increased the yield and market grade of John's Island tomatoes.

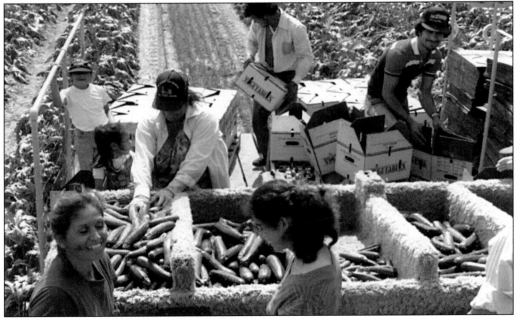

Since Florida's tomato harvest ended before South Carolina's, migrant workers followed the harvest north and arrived on the island in early summer to pick cucumbers, then tomatoes. With the decline of tomato production, many have found other types of work, made the island their home, and have contributed to the community. (Courtesy of Gene and Estelle Walpole.)

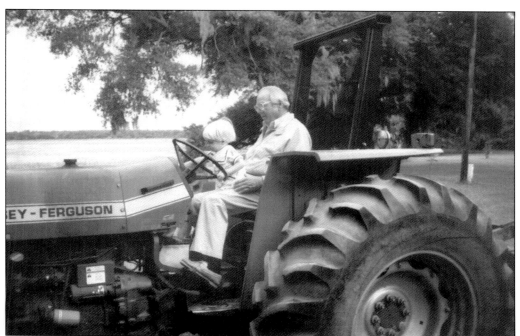

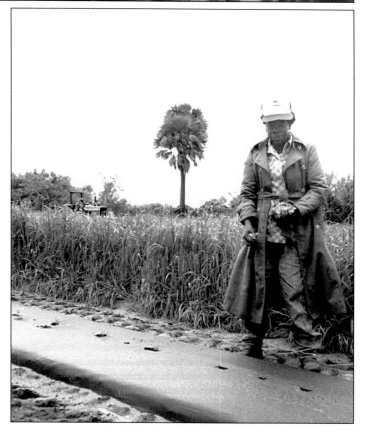

Harold Glover was one of the first farmers to plant tomatoes on John's Island. Like many farmers of his generation, he never really retired. He farmed all his life at Walnut Hill and is pictured here on his tractor with his grandson, Philip Carlton Morrow. Glover's daughter, Leize, of the fourth generation of this farming family, was the last to farm and still lives on the property. In the bottom photograph, Miss Helen, who worked for the Glovers for many years, is shown planting tomatoes. Except for the use of plastic and the advances in tractor design, basic planting methods have not changed all that much since the days of the Native Americans (see page 9). (Top, courtesy of Ethel Glover Morrow; right, courtesy of Leize Glover Bennett.)

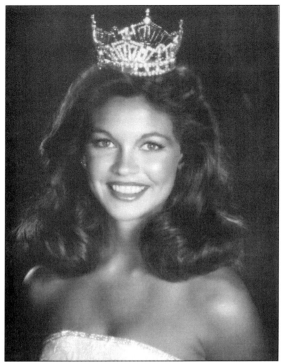

Jane Jenkins Herlong, daughter of Eleanor and Benjamin Jenkins, was named Miss South Carolina in 1980. She is now a professional speaker, award-winning singer, and author living in Johnston, South Carolina with her husband and two children. She is the author of the book *Bare Feet to High Heels: You Don't Have to be a Beauty Queen to be a Beautiful Person*. Jane claims to be fluent in four languages, "English, Southern, Northern, and Gullah." She shares humorous stories and experiences she had growing up on a farm on John's Island with many of her audiences. (Courtesy of Eleanor Jenkins.)

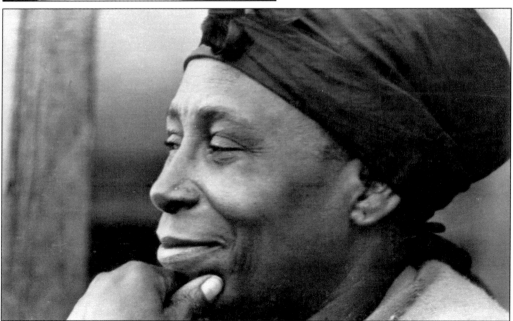

Janie Hunter lived and worked on John's Island all her life and was well known for her gift for telling folk tales. She was a lead singer for the Moving Star Hall singers and also hand crafted dolls and quilts. In 1984, she was the recipient of the National Heritage Award of the National Endowment of the Folk Arts Division. She was an active member of Wesley Methodist Church on River Road. (Courtesy of photographer Robert Yellin.)

The Moving Star Hall Singers wanted to revive interest in the spirituals and shouts handed down through generations of African Americans. Spirituals originated during slavery, when singing was a personal expression of pain and sorrow. The singers have performed at Spoleto in Charleston and the national festival of Afro-American arts in Atlanta. Pictured from left to right are Mary Pickney, Ruth "Tootsie" Bligen, Janie Hunter, and Benjamin Bligen. Members not pictured are Loretta Stanley, Bertha Smith, Yvonne Hunter, and Christine McNeil. (Photographer Robert Yellin.)

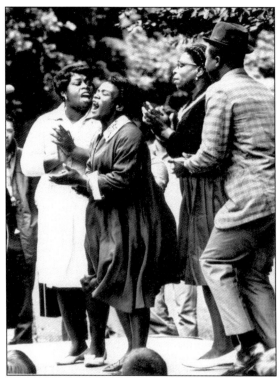

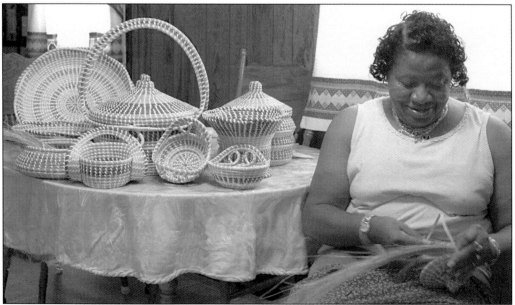

Sweetgrass used in the African basket-making craft is becoming less accessible as developments cover its habitat. Marie Wine, a third-generation sweetgrass basket maker, began learning at age six from her mother, Emily Swinton Gilliard, of Mount Pleasant. She moved to John's Island in 1975 and now sells baskets from her home and her family's stand on Highway 17 in Mount Pleasant. (Photographer Billy Rutherford.)

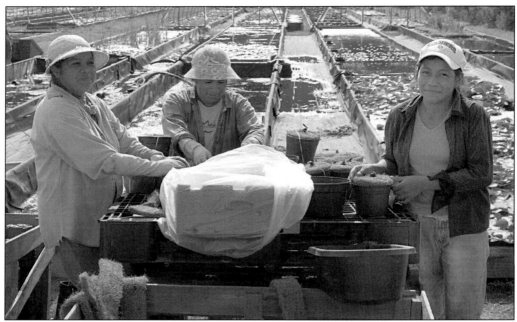

In 1986, Charleston Aquatic Nurseries opened on Canal Bridge Road. The company has become a leader in the water gardening industry, with products such as floating wetlands that control scum and growth in ponds without the use of chemicals. This wholesale business has provided new jobs for many people living on the island. These ladies are preparing the plants for the aquatic beds seen behind them. Above, from left to right, are Adela Yata, Angelina Mateo, and Oneyda Roblero. (Photographer Billy Rutherford.)

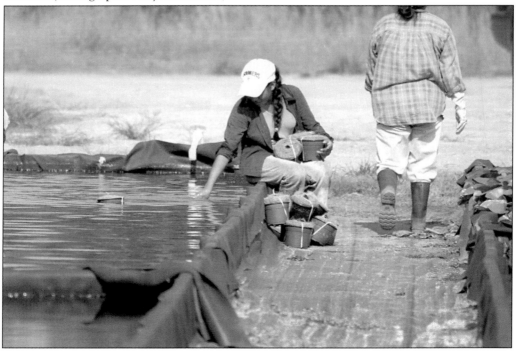

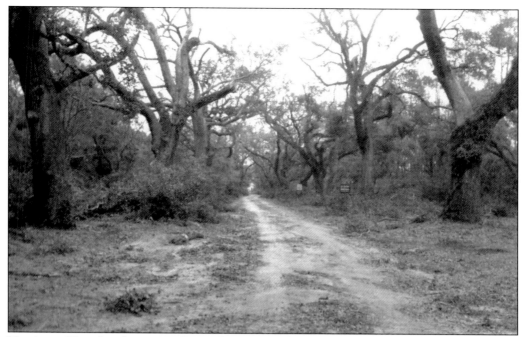

Hurricane Hugo hit the area in September 1989 with category-four winds. John's Island was on the southwest side of the storm and suffered more from wind damage than from storm surge. The tops of huge oak trees like the ones pictured here at Fenwick Hall were severely damaged by the high winds. (Courtesy of Cheryl English.)

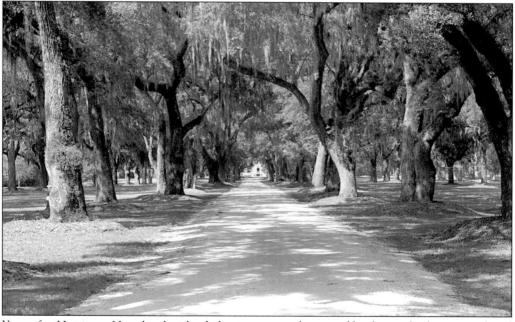

Years after Hurricane Hugo hit the island, the storm-pruned trees and landscape slowly recovered, and the familiar Spanish moss returned. The island's native live oaks, palmettos, and longleaf pine trees proved they fare better in tropical storms than other species. (Photographer Billy Rutherford.)

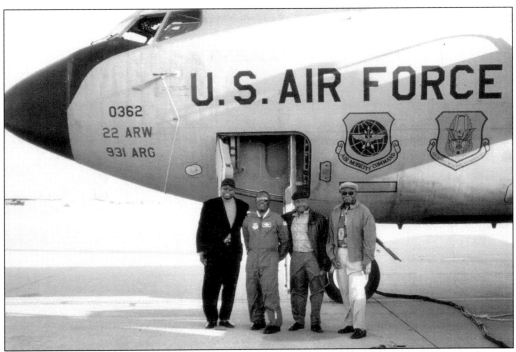

Col. William R. Saunders Jr. graduated from St. John's High School, trained at Tuskegee Institute in Alabama, became a pilot in the U.S. Air Force, and served in Desert Storm. Standing in front of the C-135 tanker he flew in 2002 are, from left to right, Cardell Jenkins, Colonel Saunders, and Eddie Fyall, a mechanical engineer with Proctor and Gamble, all of whom graduated from St. John's High School, and Bill Saunders Sr. (Courtesy of Bill Saunders.)

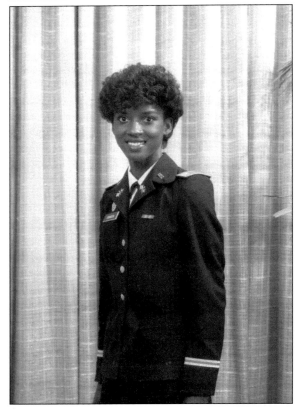

Cynthia Fields Daly, a John's Island native, graduated from the University of South Carolina in 1983 and is pictured here when she was a captain in the army in 1988. She is still on active duty and is now a lieutenant colonel. Her mother, Anna Fields White, still runs the family business, Fields' Store and Produce Stand, on South River Road. (Courtesy of Anna Fields White.)

Seven
GROWING DEVELOPMENT

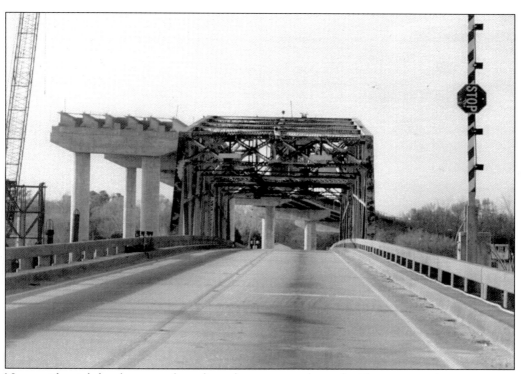

New residential developments have brought more people, and with more people comes more traffic. The island's old swing bridges had become obsolete and were replaced with bigger fixed-span, multi-lane bridges. The old Limehouse Bridge, pictured here, is overshadowed by its replacement in 2003–2004.

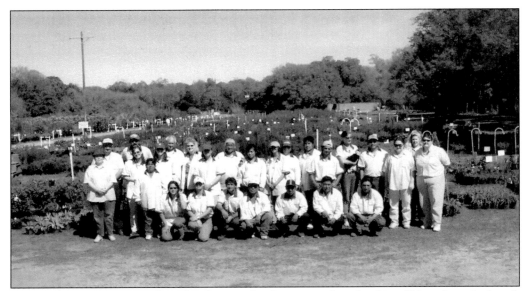

Despite the increasing number of real-estate developments, the island is still largely agricultural. The Legare family pictured here with employees has turned Hanscombe Point plantation off River Road into a sod farm, nursery, ranch, and "Farm 'N Fun" educational experience center. It also offers a corn maze in the fall, a sweet corn festival, and battle reenactments annually. The ninth generation of the Legare family is now living and working at Hanscombe Point. (Courtesy of the Legare family.)

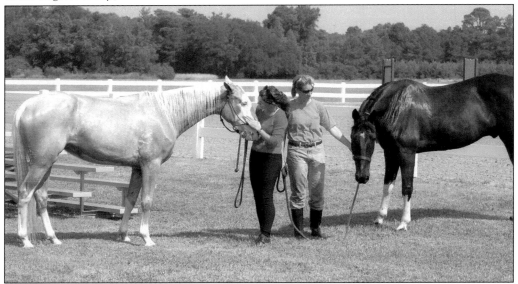

Mullet Hall, once owned by Solomon Legare and his descendants, was spared from development when Charleston County Parks Commission acquired 738 acres from the Limehouse family for the Mullet Hall Equestrian Center off South River Road. Horse enthusiasts enjoy horse shows, antique tractor shows, and festivals. There are 20 miles of moss-draped trails through pine and oak forests or open fields. April Walker (left), with her Tennessee walker Tango's Golden Angel, and Susan Hubbard (right), with Threat's Rebel, prepare for the South Carolina Pinto Horse Association Horse Show. (Photographer Billy Rutherford.)

Brick House plantation is now home to Charleston Therapeutic Riding (CATR). It is the only nationally accredited therapeutic horseback riding center in the area. A nonprofit organization, CATR provides riding programs for children and adults with disabilities. Shown with an enthusiastic participant are executive director Murray Neale (right) and a staff member. (Courtesy of Charleston Area Therapeutic Riding.)

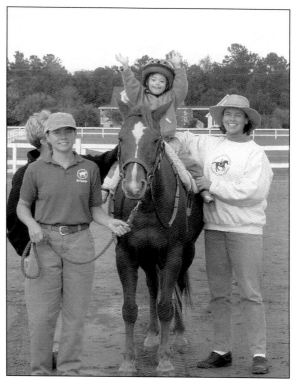

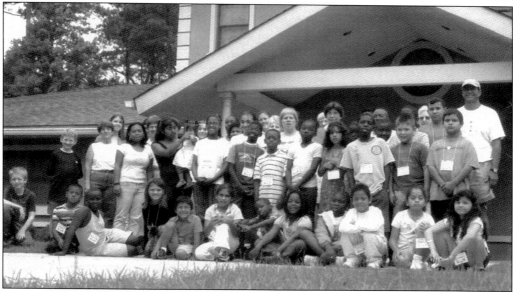

Sisters of Charity of Our Lady of Mercy was founded in 1829 by the first bishop of the Catholic diocese, Bishop John England. It became Sisters of Mercy Community Outreach Services when its mission was expanded to serve rural communities on James, John's, and Wadmalaw Islands. From its beginning in a small house on Edenvale Road just days before Hurricane Hugo hit in 1989, its services have expanded from basic emergency needs to a full-scale, bilingual community development center on Brownswood Road. (Courtesy of Sisters of Charity.)

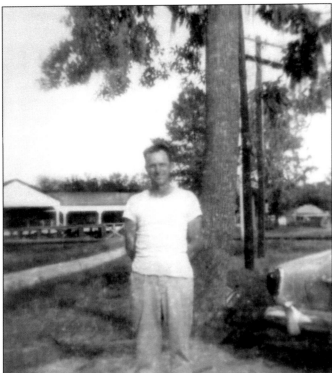

The former packing shed on Main Road is shown here to the left of Stono Depot agent Frank Howard in 1950. It was later converted to the Stono Market Café and saved as an important landmark of the former hub of agricultural commerce on the island. (Courtesy of Frank L. Howard Jr.)

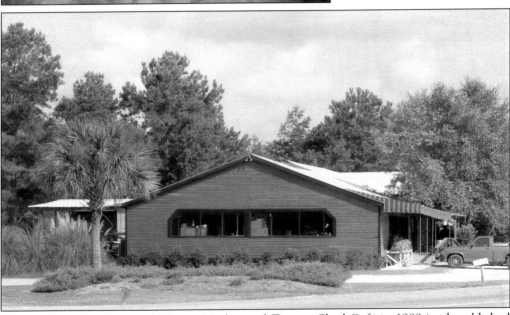

The Ambrose family opened Stono Market and Tomato Shed Café in 1989 in the old shed where produce was formerly prepared and shipped to market by train. The Ambrose family grows their own produce, used in the home-style meals found on their menu. There is also fresh local seafood, and of course, sweet tea and boiled peanuts are a given at this Southern establishment. (Photographer Billy Rutherford.)

Open-air markets have continued to gain popularity with the "comeyahs" as well as the "beenyahs." Ernest Taylor, a native islander, has been working for Rosebank Farms on Betsy Kerrison Parkway since it opened in the 1980s. Once part of an old plantation, Rosebank Farms, run by Sidi Limehouse and staff, offers a wide variety of fresh produce, flowers, local art, seafood, and a petting farm.

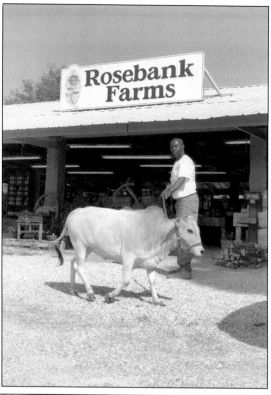

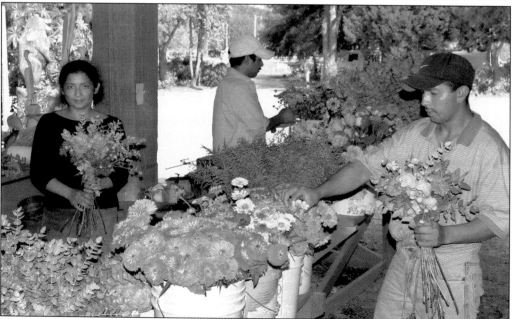

Pictured from left to right are Yolanda, Mario, and Aidely Gonzales preparing arrangements of fresh-cut flowers at Rosebank Farms. The flowers are grown in the field right next to the market. (Photographer Billy Rutherford.)

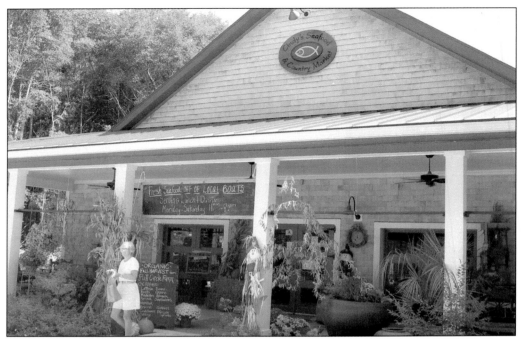

Cindy's Seafood and Country Market on Betsy Kerrison Parkway was established in 1981 by Henry and Cindy Sawyer. They have created an island ambiance using farm antiques, their fresh, organically grown vegetables, and the aroma of local seafood grilling in their country café. It is one of the few places on the island that has facilities for oyster roasts. (Photographer Billy Rutherford.)

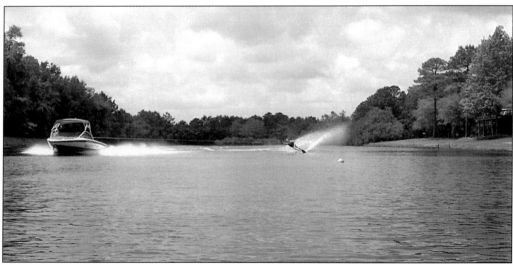

Even when the tide is out, skiing is still possible on John's Island. H2Osmosis at Trophy Lakes was built in the 1980s by Kim Bryant and Alan Sanner, and many pro-am water ski competitions have been held there for ski professionals from around the world. In the 1990s, a ski and wakeboard school was added with the help of Drew Ross. The largest lake is 275 feet wide, 2,250 feet long, and 12 to 20 deep deep, and is off Maybank Highway, tucked away in a lush pine and oak forest. (Photographer Richard Wood.)

G. Marion Reid, a descendant of Kinsey Burden and Mary Legare, retired as director of the Charleston Aviation Authority to build a horse farm on his family land, Blacklock plantation off South River Road. Stono River Stables has served John's Island and surrounding communities since 1969 with a riding school and the Lowcountry's only combined training event course. (Courtesy of Annie Caroline and Marion Reid.)

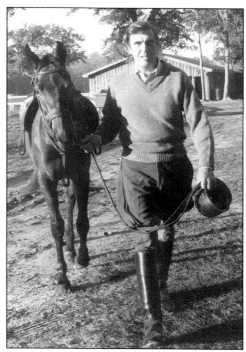

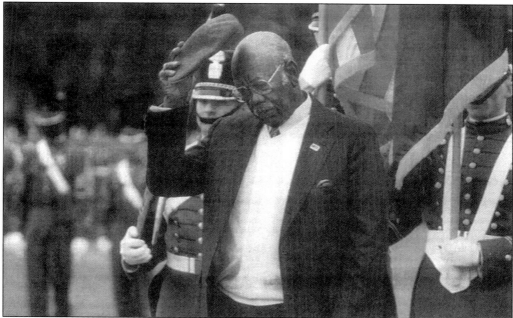

Island native William R. (Bill) Saunders Sr. has been a community leader and promoter of basic human rights most of his life. On February 7, 2003, in a ceremony at the Citadel, he was finally awarded the Purple Heart earned when he was wounded in the Korean War in 1951. For many years, he owned radio station WPAL, which was the only minority-owned station in the Charleston area. He is presently head of the Committee On Better Racial Assurance. (Courtesy of Charleston *Post and Courier*.)

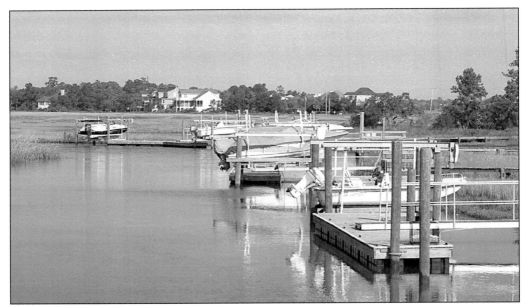

As coastal development increased throughout the Lowcountry of South Carolina, a more suburban look began to sprout on John's Island. For centuries, land-use patterns on the island reflected sparsely developed, large tracts primarily connected to agricultural use. With the expansion of the City of Charleston onto the island, development pressure, and higher demand for amenities such as waterfront lots and marsh views, more dense developments, such as these townhomes on Headquarters Island, began to change the look of John's Island.

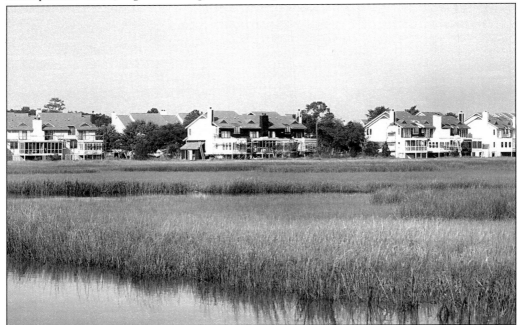

The latest crop on the island seems to be residential developments and neighborhoods. New residential units and boat lifts are seen here along Penny Creek on historic Headquarters Island. (Photographer Billy Rutherford.)

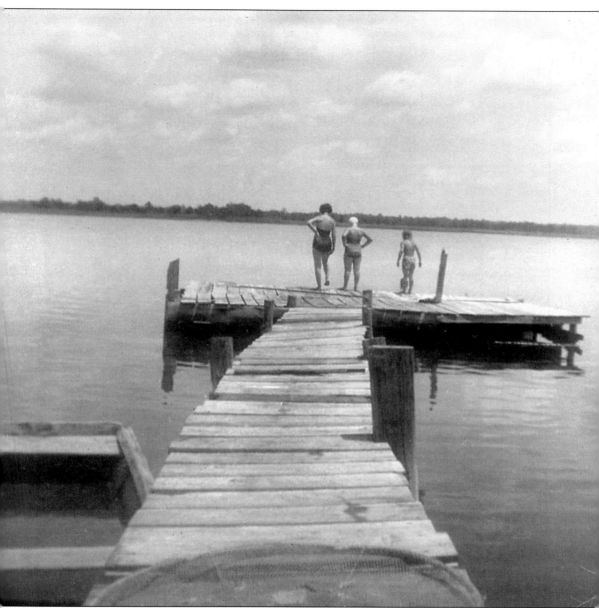

The natural landscape along the tidal rivers has drastically changed as new residential developments have grown on the island. In this 1950s photograph, island natives Nancy Limehouse (left), Carol (middle), and Margaret Seabrook enjoy a swim off an old dock in the Stono River. (Courtesy of Margaret Seabrook.)

Discover Thousands of Local History Books Featuring Millions of Vintage Images

Arcadia Publishing, the leading local history publisher in the United States, is committed to making history accessible and meaningful through publishing books that celebrate and preserve the heritage of America's people and places.

Find more books like this at
www.arcadiapublishing.com

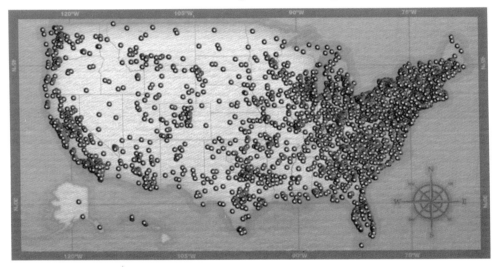

Search for your hometown history, your old stomping grounds, and even your favorite sports team.

Consistent with our mission to preserve history on a local level, this book was printed in South Carolina on American-made paper and manufactured entirely in the United States. Products carrying the accredited Forest Stewardship Council (FSC) label are printed on 100 percent FSC-certified paper.

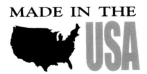